At Issue

| Political Activism

Other Books in the At Issue Series:

Alcohol Abuse

Book Banning

Bulimia

Can Diets Be Harmful?

Child Athletes

Date Rape

Does Capital Punishment Deter Crime?

Drunk Driving

Extreme Sports

Homeschooling

Human Embryo Experimentation

Is Global Warming a Threat?

Islamic Fundamentalism

Organ Transplants

Pandemics

Policing the Internet

Private Character in the Public Eye

Sexually Transmitted Diseases

Should College Athletes Be Paid?

User-Generated Content

Volunteerism

What Are the Causes of Prostitution?

What Is a Hate Crime?

Will the World Run Out of Fresh Water?

At Issue

Political Activism

Tom Lansford, Book Editor

GREENHAVEN PRESS

An imprint of Thomson Gale, a part of The Thomson Corporation

THOMSON

™

GALE

Detroit • New York • San Francisco • New Haven, Conn. • Waterville, Maine • London

Christine Nasso, *Publisher*
Elizabeth Des Chenes, *Managing Editor*

© 2008 The Gale Group.

Star logo is a trademark and Gale and Greenhaven Press are registered trademarks used herein under license.

For more information, contact:
Greenhaven Press
27500 Drake Rd.
Farmington Hills, MI 48331-3535
Or you can visit our Internet site at http://www.gale.com

LIBRARY OF CONGRESS CATALOGING-IN-PUBLICATION DATA

Political Activism / Tom Lansford, book editor.
    p. cm. -- (At issue)
Includes bibliographical references and index.
ISBN-13: 978-0-7377-3880-3 (hardcover)
ISBN-13: 978-0-7377-3881-0 (pbk.)
1. Pressure groups--United States. 2. Political activists--United States. 3. United States--Politics and government--20th century 4. Social advocacy--United States. 5. Political violence--United States. 6. Social action--United States. I. I. Lansford, Tom.
    JK1118.P64 2007
    324'.410973--dc22
                                                          2007032386

ISBN-10: 0-7377-3880-4 (hardcover)
ISBN-10: 0-7377-3881-2 (pbk.)

Printed in the United States of America
10 9 8 7 6 5 4 3 2 1

Contents

Introduction   7

1. The Government Should Support   12
   Activism Through Funding and Policy
   *John M. Bridgeland, Stephen Goldsmith, and
   Leslie Lenkowsky*

2. The Government Shouldn't Support   22
   Activism Through Funding and Policy
   Eliza Newlin Carney

3. Grassroots Organizations Are Key   33
   to Successful Political Campaigns
   Bridget Hunter

4. Outsourced Activism Has Limited Impact   38
   on Political Campaigns
   Dana R. Fisher

5. Internet Activism has Revolutionized Politics   45
   Laura D'Amelio

6. The Internet Has Revolutionized   51
   Political Campaigns
   Michael Cornfield

7. Student Activism Has Dramatically   62
   Affected American Politics
   Glenn Omatsu

8. Student Activism Has Waned in   72
   the United States
   Doug Pennington

9. Activism Has Been Crucial for the   75
   Environmental Movement
   Mark Hertsgaard

10. Activists Can Go Too Far Using Violence   **85**
    and Illegal Means to Achieve Their Aims
    John J. Miller

11. Activism Is Most Effective as a   **94**
    Grassroots Movement
    Hilda Kurtz

12. Activism Is Best When Grassroot   **103**
    Organizations Work with Local Officials
    John Baranski

Organizations to Contact   **113**
Bibliography   **119**
Index   **125**

Introduction

In the 2004 campaign, Vermont Governor Howard Dean revolutionized the presidential nominating process by redefining political activism. Dean's campaign was the first to make extensive use of the Internet. Initially regarded as a long shot who lacked national prominence or broad support within his party, Dean quickly emerged as the Democratic frontrunner but eventually lost to Massachusetts Senator John F. Kerry.

Because he lacked widespread recognition, Dean decided to try to use the Internet to interact directly with voters and to seek funds from individuals online instead of approaching wealthy groups or people for support. His message played well with grassroots activists. For instance, in a speech in South Carolina, Dean told the audience: "You have the power to rise up and take this country back. You have the power to give this party the backbone to challenge the President. . . . You have the power to create jobs, balance the budget, and bring us our dream . . . The reason people don't vote in this country is that we don't give them a reason to vote. This campaign is about giving all of you a reason to vote." Dean's opposition to the war in Iraq made him popular among the more liberal members of the Democratic Party and attracted many young people to his campaign. His supporters called themselves "Deaniacs" or "Deanites" (or even "Deany Boppers" because of their youth). For the first time in a decade, a presidential campaign drew in younger voters and encouraged their activism.

While other campaign Web sites were generally static and plain, Dean's campaign Web site, DeanforAmerica.com, was state of the art of its time. Its pages were colorful and informative and engaged people. The site featured streaming video (through what was dubbed DeanTV) of campaign events and political advertisements. Instead of paying for widespread broadcast advertising, the video component of the Web site allowed the campaign to air ads for free, and attract attention to its message through word-of-mouth. People could receive information from the campaign directly and when they wanted it, instead of the hit-or-miss tactic of airing messages on television and radio. In addition to providing information about the candidate and his views, the Web site encouraged web surfers to participate in the nominating process and communicate with other Dean supporters. Dean also developed campaign blogs, including a personal one for the candidate, Dean Blog.com, as well as one for the campaign, BlogforAmerica .com.

The Web site also contained links to other pro-Dean sites. Four were predominately featured, but there were also links to more than one hundred others. This encouraged activists to compete with one another to develop better and more popular sites, which increased Dean's presence on the web. Dean-Rocks.com was an example of one of the featured links. It was specifically targeted to young people and encouraged them to become politically active. Besides information on the Dean campaign, it also highlighted opportunities to volunteer and provided a forum to discuss major issues such as the election, global warming, and the Iraq War.

In order to connect Dean supporters with each other, the candidate's campaign manager Joe Trippi decided to use an online company, MeetUp.com to foster interaction. Trippi declared that "the largest component spreading the word—both in money and organization—are the MeetUp folks. MeetUp has been incredible. Just incredible." Such tools brought grassroots activism into the new century. MeetUp.com allowed Deaniacs to communicate with each other and organize events without employing large political organizations and therefore without paying large sums, as his competitors did. People could log on to MeetUp and enter their zip code and they would know if any events were scheduled in their area. If they wanted to network with other Deaniacs, they could use

MeetUp to arrange to get together at restaurants or coffee shops. Deaniacs could even organize their own campaign events. The grassroots-based operations proved highly effective. For instance, when Dean decided to make a brief stop in Austin, Texas, local volunteers used MeetUp to attract others. For Dean's twenty-minute speech, more than 3,200 people showed up, even though the appearance was organized in only ten days by local activists. At its height, more than 35,000 people were signed up on MeetUp.

Dean also utilized text messaging. The campaign used Upoc, a middleware company, to create a community of mobile phone users known as Dean Wireless. Subscribers received texts from the campaign that announced events or fundraising goals. In addition, like MeetUp, users could also send messages to friends or other Dean supporters and organize meetings. Within a few weeks of launching the service, Dean Wireless had 1,200 subscribers. It soon became the leading activist community on Upoc. Like MeetUp, volunteers were able to communicate with their counterparts and quickly organize events.

In many ways, the most impressive component of Dean's grassroots effort was its fundraising. In what became known as the "invisible primary" (raising campaign contributions), Dean quickly emerged as the leader within the Democratic Party. By the time the primaries commenced in 2004, Dean raised more than $50 million, surpassing previous records set by Bill Clinton in the 1996 election. Unlike his counterparts in both the Democratic and Republican parties, Dean concentrated on small donations from individuals. The average contribution was less than $80, while other candidates attempted to secure the full $2,000 allowed under federal law. This permitted the Dean campaign to seek additional donations from its supporters throughout the election.

Dean's fundraising was especially important since it was very low-cost. Internet fundraising was very low-cost com-

pared with traditional methods. Direct mailings, telephone so-
licitations, and events such as dinners, all had high overheads.
Consequently, not only did Dean raise more money, but his
campaign spent less to get it and was therefore able to devote
more of the resources into getting his message out. The
campaign's contributions were recorded online through what
became a famous image: the campaign bat. This page on the
Web site featured a baseball player holding a bat with the
phrase "You gotta believe!" superimposed on the image. As
more contributions came in, a line on the bat moved upward,
demonstrating progress toward a specific goal. As goals were
met, additional bats were added. Dean also entertained sug-
gestions from contributors. For example, he allowed supporters to vote on whether or not he would accept federal matching funds in the primary elections (doing so would have meant
limitations on what the campaign could spend). Voters over-
whelmingly rejected the idea of matching funds, allowing
Dean to spend more.

Dean emerged as the frontrunner in the Democratic primaries as a result of his innovative strategy of relying on Internet activism. However, his campaign unraveled after the
Iowa Caucus, the first state polling. Dean placed third in the
voting and then compounded his loss in an appearance in
which he punctuated a speech with a scream. Dean ended by
declaring that "we're going to Washington, D.C., to take back
the White House. Yeeeeaaagh." The so-called "Dean Scream"
made many people uncomfortable and made the candidate
appear out of control during the address (Dean later attributed the scream to over-enthusiasm and the fact that he was
unaware that a microphone was broadcasting the speech, and
he did not, therefore, need to raise his voice). Kerry quickly
overtook Dean as the leader of the party. Kerry was eventually
defeated by Republican George W. Bush in November 2004.

Dean's innovative use of the Internet changed the nature
of political activism in the United States. Many of the strate-

gies used by the campaign were later replicated by others in subsequent elections. Nevertheless, the reasons that people became involved in grassroots efforts remained constant, as did the willingness of individuals to band together to influence and implement policies. Such efforts remain the core of American democracy.

The Government Should Support Activism Through Funding and Policy

John M. Bridgeland, Stephen Goldsmith, and Leslie Lenkowsky

John M. Bridgeland is the assistant to the president and director of the Office of USA Freedom Corps. Stephen Goldsmith is the chairman of the Board of the Corporation for National and Community Service and the author of Putting Faith in Neighborhoods. *Leslie Lenkowsky is the chief executive officer of the Corporation for National and Community Service.*

President George W. Bush has endeavored to increase citizen activism and community service through expanded government support for civic programs and the creation of the USA Freedom Corps. Bush has attempted to harness the power and influence of private activist groups to address national issues such as homeland security, public health and disaster relief. The administration hoped to mobilize grassroots "armies of compassion" to supplement governmental efforts by empowering local groups to deal with what matters were most pressing to the community. Bush's initiatives have resulted in increased volunteerism and community activism.

From his first major speech as a presidential candidate, in Indianapolis in July 1999, George W. Bush has made expanding civic engagement and increasing the strength and ef-

John M. Bridgeland, Stephen Goldsmith, and Leslie Lenkosky, "New Directions: Service and the Bush Administration's Civic Agenda," *The Brookings Review*, vol. 20, Fall 2002, pp. 18–21. Copyright 2002 Brookings Institution. Reproduced by permission.

fectiveness of civic institutions a central aim. He articulated his vision for an active and engaged citizenry in his inaugural address, in which he urged Americans to be "citizens, not spectators; citizens, not subjects; responsible citizens, building communities of service and a nation of character."

Bush and National Service

The events of September 11 added energy and urgency to this goal, as an active citizenry became an important bulwark against terrorist threats. These policy aims took their most concrete form in the 2002 State of the Union address, when President Bush called on all Americans to devote at least two years—or 4,000 hours—over their lifetimes in service to their communities, nation, and world. The president announced he had created the USA Freedom Corps to promote and coordinate government and private-sector efforts to give Americans more meaningful service opportunities to answer that call. As part of the USA Freedom Corps he also formed Citizen Corps to help citizens play appropriate roles in meeting the nation's emerging homeland defense needs and called for expanding the Peace Corps, Senior Corps, and AmeriCorps.

The president's embrace of national service programs, while springing directly from his philosophy of compassionate conservatism, no doubt surprised many people who had come to associate such efforts with Democratic presidents. Few people dispute that the voluntary efforts of citizens can make neighborhoods safer, the environment cleaner, children more prepared to face life's challenges, seniors healthier, and communities better able to deal with emergencies. But the challenge for many has been to define the role government ought to play in this arena. Can federally funded service be administered in a way that protects the independence of the civic sector and ensures that citizens, rather than government, take responsibility for the health and safety of their neighborhoods and their nation?

Activism and Democracy

A long tradition in American politics warns against allowing government to encroach on the private sector. No less a student of American democracy than Alexis de Tocqueville warned that the growth of government could weaken the American tradition of joining civic groups. In the 1950s, sociologist Robert Nisbet, among others, lamented the decline of community, blaming it on the destructive effects of an expanding welfare state. Recently, a host of figures, especially Robert Putnam in his book *Bowling Alone*, have warned that Americans are reaching dangerous levels of civic disengagement, one measure of which is declining interest in volunteering and civic associations.

Not until 1965, however, did many thinkers who were concerned about government encroachment on the voluntary sector begin to develop a positive agenda for the diffuse web of nonprofit groups, associations, schools, and community organizations that came to be known as the "independent sector." Chief among them was Richard Cornuelle, a businessman and political activist, who in his 1965 book, *Reclaiming the American Dream*, challenged the right to demonstrate how private, nonprofit organizations could successfully tackle tasks such as making a college education affordable to the lower and middle classes, reducing poverty and welfare dependency, and improving housing for the needy. Could developing an agenda for the independent sector, he asked, offer a way to address pressing public needs without expanding government?

How to Empower People

A decade later, two scholars from the American Enterprise Institute, Peter Berger and Richard John Neuhaus, set out such an agenda. They urged government to make better use of "mediating structures"—neighborhood, family, church, and voluntary associations—to deal with social problems. In their widely discussed "To Empower People," they set forth two propositions: first, that government policy should stop harming these mediating structures and, second, that it should use them whenever possible to realize social purposes.

During Governor Bush's campaign for the presidency, his support for mediating structures and the people they mobilize—now termed "armies of compassion"—figured prominently. He proposed to clear away legal and bureaucratic obstacles, thereby allowing the federal government to provide support to grassroots groups, exactly the kind of mediating institutions that Berger and Neuhaus had in mind.

... the President called on all Americans to devote at least two years during their lifetimes to serving their neighbors and their nation.

In Bush's vision, federal service programs fill a special niche—they create more opportunities for people to volunteer. Through AmeriCorps, for example, the intensive commitment members make—up to 40 hours a week for one or two years—would be directed to helping organizations locate, train, and mobilize the armies of compassion.

September 11 and Activism

In the fall of 2001, the administration was hoping to advance its strategy for citizen engagement through a "Communities of Character" initiative. The president was planning to spotlight places across the nation where people voluntarily came together to solve problems, putting others' interests above their own. The attacks on September 11 made that effort superfluous. Communities across the United States sent medical and relief teams to New York and Washington, while millions of ordinary citizens donated blood and money. "What can I do to help?" became an almost universal refrain, making citizenship and service more important than ever. In response, the president announced plans to increase the role of AmeriCorps members and Senior Corps volunteers in public safety, public health, and disaster relief and to focus their efforts more sharply on homeland security.

In his 2002 State of the Union message, the two halves of the Bush administration's civic agenda came together. Toward the end of an address devoted chiefly to the war against terrorism, homeland security, and the economy, the president called on all Americans to devote at least two years during their lifetimes to serving their neighbors and their nation. Acts of goodness and compassion in one's community, he argued, would be an appropriate way of responding to the "evils" of September 11. And he proposed changes in national service programs to enable more Americans to serve both through these programs and through the grassroots organizations they would support.

These proposals represent a new direction in national and community service. To begin with, they put to rest the idea— which has gained currency in the aftermath of September 11—that national and community service should be made mandatory. Whether in AmeriCorps, the Peace Corps, or in private organizations, service, the president said, was to continue to be a voluntary, individual, moral commitment.

The proposed reforms also make clear that service through the federal government is to strengthen, not replace, traditional volunteering. The president anticipated that most Americans would answer his "call to service" by continuing to devote a few hours a week to work with a local church, school, hospital, or nonprofit. But federal programs like AmeriCorps and the Peace Corps would be available for those who wanted an intensive volunteer experience at home or abroad. The president also directed various cabinet departments to explore ways to encourage more Americans to volunteer and to remove any barriers to participation.

The Role of the Federal Government

In the administration's vision of national service, participants take on tasks different from those performed by ordinary volunteers. Volunteerism is not free, in the sense that volunteers must be recruited, organized, and set to work. To make more effective the efforts of millions of individual volunteers, who come to the table with all types of skills, abilities, and experiences, someone has to organize volunteer opportunities so that they meet concrete and clearly defined human needs. The organizations mobilizing the "armies of compassion" need corporals and sergeants—precisely the role that this administration sees for national service participants. Whether in education, the environment, public health, elder care, or strengthening homeland security, their long-term commitment is of special value to charities and public agencies, which can count on them to show up each day, receive training, and take on long-range tasks and responsibilities that ordinary volunteers cannot—something known in the nonprofit world as "capacity building." That difference also justifies paying some of them a small stipend for living expenses, as well as a GI Bill-type award for education.

Habitat for Humanity already follows this approach. It uses AmeriCorps members and Senior Corps volunteers to recruit, manage, and organize the traditional volunteers on which it relies to build homes for low-income people. Habitat founder Millard Fuller—once skeptical of AmeriCorps, but now an enthusiastic supporter—reports that volunteer leveraging by AmeriCorps members serving with Habitat has helped the group build 2,000 extra homes and engage more than 250,000 new volunteers. AmeriCorps members working with Habitat do not replace the volunteers who are building the houses; instead, they help recruit them from college campuses and elsewhere. They also ready the building sites so that when the hammer-swinging volunteers show up, they can get right to work and have a more productive experience. Along

with helping Habitat build more houses, AmeriCorps participants thus engage more Americans in civic activities.

AmeriCorps and Freedom Corps

Another version of this model is to use AmeriCorps members
to build the administrative and technological capacities of
grassroots groups. For example, since it was created in 1965,
members of Volunteers in Service to America (VISTA), who
now make up about 15 percent of AmeriCorps members, have
focused their efforts on mobilizing and managing teams of
volunteer counselors, developing or expanding programs, and
implementing administrative and accounting systems. Those
efforts equip nonprofits—or voluntary public health or disaster relief groups—to do more of the work they already do.
This fall, for example, VISTA will fund 10 members to work
with Students in Free Enterprise (SIFE) at strategic points
around the country, helping to develop SIFE teams that will
teach financial literacy, from balancing checkbooks to investment strategies, to underprivileged populations in inner cities.
The VISTA members won't do the actual teaching; rather, they
will expand the program by training and developing new
teams.

Implementing these strategies requires changing not only
how federal service programs have been run, but also the laws
establishing them. While VISTA members, for example, are allowed to do a wide range of capacity-building activities, other
AmeriCorps participants, governed by rules enacted in the
1990s, are now required by law to provide services (such as
tutoring or health care) directly to clients. Changes to allow
national service participants to perform a wider range of services were incorporated in a set of principles for a Citizen Service Act, which the Bush administration unveiled last spring.
The bill, which includes reforms to mobilize more volunteers
who receive nothing from government, to make organizations

receiving support more effective and accountable, and to remove barriers to participation in service programs, is now before Congress.

Finally, the president will use his new White House council, the USA Freedom Corps, to promote the health of the voluntary sector in general. The council will not only coordinate the efforts of all volunteer and service programs in the federal tent, but also concern itself with federal policies that affect the well-being of civil society. For example, it can work across federal agencies to improve the effectiveness of school tutoring programs that help students in need. And it can encourage organizations—businesses and nonprofits alike—to respond to the president's call to service by making institutional changes, such as giving employees paid time off for service, enlisting consumers in volunteer service activities, and increasing the capacity of service providers to use volunteers. For the first time, at the highest levels of our government, a presidential council will develop an agenda of "citizenship, service, and responsibility."

Since the president's call to service, interest in volunteer and national service is up.

The USA Freedom Corps will link citizens with service opportunities in their communities. In July, the president unveiled a redesigned website that features the USA Freedom Corps Volunteer Network, the largest clearinghouse of volunteer opportunities ever created. Thanks to an unprecedented collaboration among many government agencies, for-profit companies, nonprofit organizations, and private foundations, Americans can now find volunteer opportunities anywhere in the country (and even abroad) with just a few clicks of the mouse. The effort represents the power of government to rally diverse (and sometimes competitive) groups to a higher and shared purpose—and offers a glimpse of the public-private partnerships that are possible when government promotes service.

Federal Support for Service

Since the president's call to service, interest in volunteer and national service is up. Key indicators include the increase in the numbers of citizens being matched with local service opportunities, as well as traffic at web sites for the USA Freedom Corps and the recruitment websites of Senior Corps and AmeriCorps, where applications have more than doubled. The Peace Corps also reports steady increases in applications. Nonprofit organizations, businesses, schools, faith-based groups, and other institutions are stepping forward to answer the call to service with new commitments and, in many cases, institutional changes that promise to foster a culture of service for years to come.

The Bush administration's civic agenda, together with its reform of national service, represents an unprecedented, cross-sector push to reconnect Americans to their communities and their country—and a new direction in how government views its role in strengthening the voluntary sector. Instead of bemoaning the decline of American mediating institutions, the administration seeks public actions to reinvigorate them. In an era of a high-tech, low-manpower military, it also looks for ways to involve as many Americans as possible in serving their country during a time of war and to encourage institutional changes at every level to ensure that volunteer service remains strong in times of peace. It aims to provide avenues for Americans, especially young adults and senior citizens able to offer sustained volunteer service, to dedicate themselves to reaching out and ministering to the needy and suffering. The president's service agenda clearly reflects the belief that citizens who are closest to the needs of people in local communities are best positioned to bring hope and help to those most needing it and that a renewed effort is needed to mobilize more Americans into volunteer service.

In identifying national and community service as a force for institutional and cultural renewal, the Bush administration has begun to make it an idea that Americans of all political stripes can embrace.

2

The Government Shouldn't Support Activism Through Funding and Policy

Eliza Newlin Carney

Eliza Newlin Carney is a contributing editor for the National Journal *and a freelance author who writes extensively about American politics and society.*

President George W. Bush initiated a broad federal effort to provide financial and other support for private volunteer organizations in an effort to improve community service. However, the initiative was not very well-developed and government agencies have encountered a number of hurdles and challenges in their efforts to help civic bodies. In addition, the focus of the efforts on faith-based organizations has raised a number of legal and constitutional concerns over the division between church and state. Consequently, even some conservatives and religious leaders are uncomfortable with the approach. Meanwhile, concerns have arisen over accountability and oversight of federal funding for private groups.

When Jim Towey signed on as director of the White House Office of Faith-Based and Community Initiatives [in 2002], he had a few basic questions. "I came in and I said: Well, how many faith-based organizations even get federal money?" Towey recalls asking. "How much money do they get? Which programs are they involved in? Do they do a good

Eliza Newlin Carney, "Leap of Faith," *Government Executive*, vol. 35, no. 7, June 2003. Reproduced by permission.

job or not?" Nobody could tell him a thing. As Towey describes it, the response he got was: "We don't know any of those answers. We couldn't tell you." Towey, who formerly headed Florida's health and social services agency, was dumbfounded. "How can you measure the success of any initiative if you don't have basic data?"

Towey, like many administration officials working on President Bush's faith-based initiative, has discovered that doling out federal money to faith-based groups is more complicated than it sounds. Two and a half years after President Bush announced it as an urgent priority, the initiative to federally fund faith-based and community groups has proved controversial, ambitious—and surprisingly difficult to administer.

Faith-Based Activism

The theory seems simple enough. Convinced that faith-based groups, in particular, have been unfairly excluded from the federal grants system, Bush has launched a multi-part effort to level the playing field. He announced the creation of the first-ever White House Office for Faith-Based and Community Initiatives during his first week in office. He pushed hard for legislation to ease federal restrictions on faith-based groups. He issued executive orders establishing new federal rules for faith-based charities and launching centers for Faith-Based and Community Initiatives at seven government agencies.

The lack of knowledge about faith-based groups is a major stumbling block.

But in practice, bringing more faith-based groups under the federal umbrella has proved problematic at best. The White House office got off to a rocky start, and was publicly excoriated for valuing politics over policy by its first director, political scientist John Dilulio Jr. Dilulio later publicly apologized for telling *Esquire* magazine in a January 2002 article that "everything" in the White House was "being run by the political arm." Legislation to help faith-based groups has foundered on Capitol Hill, leaving the administration to forge ahead with only lukewarm support in Congress.

Problems with the Initiatives

Agency officials implementing the plan have stumbled into numerous gray areas and political land mines. Many lack even a clear definition of what constitutes a faith-based organization. Federal agencies rely on states, localities and intermediaries to distribute grants, but that often leaves them several steps removed from the grantees. Agencies, moreover, have no additional money to hand out to new groups; they will simply be dividing the existing pie into smaller slices.

Lack of knowledge about faith-based groups is a major stumbling block. Bush and his allies have collected many a heartwarming anecdote to trumpet the success of faith-based charities. But scholars have yet to produce reliable data on the actual performance of such organizations. The disparate nature of faith-based and community groups, their frequently small size, volunteer staffs and mission-driven management style have made them hard to study.

Those same factors will make it especially hard for federal officials to track, monitor and assess the performance of these organizations. "When you federalize a program like this, it presents major problems in terms of monitoring," says Kathryn Dunn Tenpas, a guest scholar at the Brookings Institution who wrote a report on the Office of Faith-Based and Community Initiatives. Baylor University professor Gaynord Yancey concurs. "Government traditionally has been used to working with the bigger umbrella organizations," says Yancey. "To get down to those who are in urban neighborhoods, who are beneath the radar screen . . . is going to be the major, major challenge for government."

Traditional Funding

To be sure, the federal government has publicly funded some types of faith-based organizations for decades. National organizations such as Catholic Charities USA, United Jewish Communities and the Salvation Army long have been partners with an array of agencies to deliver social services. Catholic Charities, for example, gets more than half of its funding from government grants.

But the president's faith-based initiative is breaking significant new ground. In the past, religious organizations were required to secularize their social service activities, so they were separate in time and place from their religious activities, in order to get public funds. This practice dated to as early as the 1970s, when Supreme Court rulings barred faith-based groups from receiving direct government support for inherently religious activities. Often this meant that a sponsoring religious institution had to incorporate as a separate tax-exempt group, or charitable arm, to carry out its social services.

That began to change in 1996, when President Clinton signed sweeping welfare reform legislation that included "charitable choice" provisions allowing religious groups to seek federal funding for some programs without having to change their religious character or governance. Under charitable choice, a faith-based group receiving federal welfare grants no longer must set up a separate charitable arm to deliver social services. The new charitable choice welfare rules also allow social service providers to maintain a religious environment at their facilities—displaying crosses or retaining a religious name, for example. In addition, entities that receive federal contracts may consider religious beliefs in their hiring and firing decisions.

The Bush Program

Bush now has applied the charitable choice model to all federal agencies. While the administration has taken pains to in-

25

clude community groups in its initiative, there's little doubt that Bush's real interest is in the healing power of religion to help people overcome poverty, addiction and other social ills. "Faith-based charities work daily miracles because they have idealistic volunteers," Bush declared in a Philadelphia speech in December announcing his two most recent executive orders implementing the initiative. "They're guided by moral principles. They know the problems of their own communities, and above all, they recognize the dignity of every citizen and the possibilities of every life."

The first executive order issued in Philadelphia established centers for Faith-Based and Community Initiatives at the Agriculture Department and the Agency for International Development. Such centers had been created by an executive order issued Jan. 29, 2001, at the departments of Health and Human Services, Housing and Urban Development, Education, Justice and Labor. The second Philadelphia order imposed charitable choice provisions on the full spectrum of federal social service programs. It specified, for example, that faith-based groups should be able to compete for grants "on a level playing field" with nonreligious providers without having to change their religious character.

The president's faith-based rhetoric has alarmed critics, who warn that the new rules will breach the constitutional wall dividing church and state. They object to religious congregations receiving direct federal funding. Even more controversial is the provision to allow groups to hire and fire on the basis of religion, which reverses part of an executive order issued by President Johnson in 1965 prohibiting discrimination by entities that have federal procurement contracts.

Congressional Concerns

In 2001, the House approved a bill to essentially codify Bush's faith-based initiative, but it died in the Senate. In April, the Senate approved the Charity, Aid, Recovery and Empowerment (CARE) Act, but only after its sponsors abandoned all substantive faith-based provisions, including one that would have allowed religious charities to compete for federal grants without altering their religious character. The legislation was stripped down to a tax bill that encourages charitable donations.

The faith-based initiative raises serious performance and accountability questions for people on both sides of the constitutional debate.

At the same time, some social scientists, academics and social service providers embrace the Bush initiative as a logical next step in delivering social services. The administration's effort has tapped a well of growing interest in forming innovative new partnerships between government and community and religious groups. "The faith-based debate fits into that larger question about how can government be more agile, be more creative in working with other institutions," says Luis Lugo, director of the Religion Program at the Pew Charitable Trusts, a Philadelphia-based organization that provides grants for nonprofit activities. Faith-based and community groups are potential government partners "on the ground, that are trusted by the people they are trying to serve, and that generate significant resources," Lugo notes.

The faith-based initiative raises serious performance and accountability questions for people on both sides of the constitutional debate. The initiative could steer billions of federal dollars to an array of unknown, untested groups that have no experience working with the government. It spans multiple agencies and literally hundreds of programs, making funding available for everything from after-school tutoring to soup kitchens, drug treatment, homeless shelters, job training and transitional help for ex-convicts.

Faith-Based Groups

What is a faith-based organization? A basic problem for agency officials is that there's no simple answer. A faith-based organization could be a religious program housed in a congregation. It could be a nonprofit affiliated with a religious group. It could be a nonreligious program staffed by people of faith. It could be a partnership between religious and secular groups. The permutations are endless, and administrative questions vary with the nature of the group.

"Lack of clarity in our vocabulary on this subject creates problems for studying, funding and making policies regarding social service and educational entities with a connection to religion," concludes a recent report by the Working Group on Human Needs and Faith-Based and Community Initiatives, a coalition of policy experts, activists and religious leaders. The working group is coordinated by the Search for Common Ground USA, a Washington-based nonprofit devoted to conflict prevention and resolution. The hazy distinction between religious congregations and faith-based groups has landed the Housing and Urban Development Department [(HUD)] in an emotional controversy. HUD has proposed regulations that would allow an organization to use federal funds to renovate facilities that are sometimes used for worship and sometimes for social services. Civil liberties groups and some on Capitol Hill have criticized the regulations.

Lack of Public Support

Concern about the potential ill effects of federal support has led some conservatives and religious leaders to reject the Bush model. What makes religious programs so effective, some argue, is that they are free from government intrusion and red tape. "Officials in faith-based charities may end up spending more time reading the *Federal Register* than the Bible," warns Michael Tanner, director of health and welfare studies at the libertarian Cato Institute, in a March 2001 critique of the Bush initiative dubbed "Corrupting Charity."

An administrative challenge for the faith-based initiative is that federal agencies do not, in most cases, directly fund faith-based and community groups and therefore rely on state and local officials or intermediary organizations to collect data necessary to ensure accountability and assess results. Most of the money goes through block grants or formula grants to the states. It could then pass through local governments or intermediaries, on whom federal officials rely heavily to help smaller groups navigate the system.

For example, last year, the Labor Department gave out $17.5 million in grants to states and to intermediaries to encourage them to reach out to faith-based and community groups. Labor asked the intermediaries, in particular, to propose how to link smaller, grassroots organizations with the 1998 Workforce Investment Act system, which runs federal job training programs. The theory is that larger umbrella groups (an example would be Catholic Charities) can take administrative and reporting burdens off smaller ones. "You really need more experienced organizations who can serve as the administrative body for some of the smaller ones," says Brent Orrell, director of the Labor Department's Center for Faith-Based and Community Initiatives. "It just doesn't make sense to go around building administrative capacity in all of these smaller organizations. They need the economies of scale, which all of the intermediaries bring."

Problems with Intermediaries

But some intermediaries have come under fire. Last year, the Health and Human Services [(HHS)] Department drew criticism when it awarded a $500,000 grant to Operation Blessing International, an organization led by controversial religious leader Pat Robertson, who repeatedly has been criticized for disparaging gays and lesbians, feminists and Jews. Operation

Blessing was one of several intermediaries asked to distribute sub-grants to smaller faith-based and community groups to help them build capacity and manage their programs more effectively. The money came from the HHS Compassion Capital Fund, which aims to give faith-based and community groups the technical training they need to apply for and meet the requirements of federal grants. The fund doled out 21 grants totaling $24.5 million for such training in fiscal 2002. Some $35 million has been appropriated for the fund in fiscal 2003, and Bush wants to increase that to $100 million in the coming fiscal year.

Relying on intermediaries can make federal money harder to track, skeptics warn. "It's not clear at this point who's getting the money and what they're doing with it [and] what kinds of results they're getting," says Kay Guinane, counsel and manager of community education at OMB Watch, a Washington-based watchdog group focusing on government accountability and civic participation. Using intermediaries raises questions about "what kind of financial and programmatic accountability system will be put in place," she adds. Such problems can be avoided, Towey maintains, "if you make it clear that the intermediaries are as accountable for the sub-award activity as they are for their own activity." He and other administration officials stress that the standards for performance, certification and accountability are the same for faith-based and community groups as they are for any federal grantees.

Some social service providers also protest that there's a drastic mismatch between what Bush calls the "armies of compassion" and the available funding.

"I don't think that the issue of accountability and management of grants going to faith-based groups is really any different than the management of grants going to other social service providers, who aren't faith-based," says Towey.

Indeed, faith-based and community groups have no guarantee they will receive federal grants under the initiative. The administration has set aside no significant new money for such organizations. HHS' Compassion Capital Fund does introduce some seed money, but it underwrites training and recruitment, not direct services. Some investments are associated with the initiative, including $600 million for drug treatment vouchers. But the initiative largely calls on agencies to encourage new grantees within existing budgets.

Funding Uncertainty

The absence of special faith-based funding creates its own challenges. Agency officials will not have the money to underwrite new grassroots organizations, as Bush has directed them to do, unless they cut the funding for current grantees. In some cases this may mean abandoning a larger, well-known charity with a proven track record in order to take a risk on an unfamiliar, less-experienced organization. This has alarmed some well-established social service providers, who worry about unfair competition. "The concern is that the agenda here is to prefer particular groups . . . that preference flies in the face of equal standards, equal opportunity," says Diana Aviv, president of Independent Sector, a coalition of national voluntary and philanthropic organizations.

Some social service providers also protest that there's a drastic mismatch between what Bush call the "armies of compassion" and the available funding. The CARE Act includes a $1.3 billion increase in social service block grant funding to states, but Bush objects to that feature of the bill. Yet White House and agency officials continue to host standing-room-only forums in major cities to encourage faith-based and community groups to apply for federal grants. "Without additional funding, it's a cruel hoax to run around the country encouraging people to apply for funds that aren't there," said Mary Nelson, president of Bethel New Life, a faith-based community development corporation in Chicago. Nelson spoke at an April [2003] conference in Washington on harnessing the power of faith-based and community groups.

3

Grassroots Organizations Are Key to Successful Political Campaigns

Bridget Hunter

Bridget Hunter is a staff writer for the United States Department of State's international information programs. Ms. Hunter contributes frequently to the Washington File, the daily news service for the State Department. Her columns address both domestic and international issues.

American elections would not be possible without the hard work and dedication of political activists. These citizens provide a range of services and support to individual candidates, political parties, and the governmental bodies overseeing balloting. These mostly unpaid volunteers typically begin working for campaigns months prior to the actual polling and distribute campaign literature and canvas on behalf of candidates. Concurrently, nonpartisan activist groups attempt to inform voters of both sides of an issue and increase turn-out on election-day. Finally, nonpartisan volunteers also serve as election officials on the day of the balloting after undergoing training by government officials. Partisan and nonpartisan activists provide these necessary services to ensure the smooth functioning of American elections.

Bright balloons bob above a sea of rainbow-colored signs as loudspeakers blare music and announcements, and people in hats and shirts emblazoned with slogans hand out

Bridget Hunter, "U.S. Election Day a Celebration of Political Activism," U.S. State Department UNINFO, November 3, 2006. U.S. Department of State, Washington, DC.

flyers, stickers and buttons. Election Day in the United States often arrives dressed as a carnival, ready to attract attention and excite voter interest.

Election Day

The day begins early. On November 7, [2006] in villages, towns and cities across the United States, thousands of volunteers will rise before dawn to lend a hand during the U.S. midterm elections. Some will line up outside campaign headquarters, eager to pick up the flyers, pamphlets and signs they will distribute at polling places in the hope of still influencing voters' decisions.

Others will go directly to the school cafeterias, gymnasiums and community centers that serve as polling places to assist in checking voter rolls, setting up voting machines and ensuring the elections are conducted in accordance with all applicable laws and regulations.

For these dedicated volunteers, Election Day is the culmination of months of hard work—a day when volunteers of all ages and backgrounds enjoy the excitement and occasional chaos of democracy in action.

The Importance of Activists

A campaign worker's involvement might have started with a newspaper article, a call for help from a community group or labor union, or a chance meeting with a prospective candidate. It might have been an issue on which he or she felt passionately that prompted a voter to give a candidate more than just a vote on Election Day. Whatever their initial reason for getting involved, these volunteers, most of them unpaid, lend their time and expertise to inform, educate and encourage their fellow voters to support specific candidates, political parties or issues.

Their involvement is essential to the U.S. election process. Most political organizations in the United States rely heavily on unpaid volunteers to mount effective campaigns, and both parties actively recruit volunteers on national, state and local levels.

The Republican National Committee's Web site calls for volunteers to become the party's link to their communities and "to spread the party's message as well as garner support for candidates and the president's and our party's agenda."

The Democratic National Committee offers specific advice for the week preceding Election Day: "See if your local campaign needs any help Thursday or Friday night," its Web site directs. "Since you will be at the campaign headquarters all weekend, buy granola bars, fruit, and water today for the campaign staff and volunteers."

Functions of Volunteers

In the United States, campaign workers perform a variety of tasks to promote their candidates' messages and get out the vote:

- "Lit drops" involve distributing by hand printed literature about a candidate to voters' homes, with volunteers assigned a specific area.

- "Canvassing" involves knocking on the doors of homes to talk with voters.

- "Mailers" are campaign literature sent to voters' homes, but volunteers prepare the material—folding letters and stuffing, stamping and addressing envelopes.

- "Phone-banking" involves hundreds, sometimes thousands, of phone calls to prospective voters, promoting candidates and encouraging participation in the election.

Months in advance of the election, volunteers start distributing signs for voters to place in their windows or yards and handing out literature at bus and subway stops. They attend rallies and fundraising events; wear T-shirts with campaign slogans and display flags and bumper stickers on their cars— all to demonstrate support for the candidates of their choice.

On Election Day, volunteers distribute campaign literature and voter information at polling places and serve as their parties' witnesses to the legal conduct of voting. A long day's work (sometimes more than 12 hours at the polls) is capped by an anxious wait at a "victory" party for news of whether their candidate won or lost the election.

Nonpartisan Volunteers

Many other volunteers working on Election Day take a deliberately nonpartisan approach and work to educate rather than influence voters.

Members of the League of Women Voters, a nonpartisan political organization established in 1920, are dedicated to improving government and enhancing public policy through citizen education. The organization describes itself as "a grassroots organization, working at the national, state and local levels" throughout the United States and its territories. Strictly nonpartisan, it neither supports nor opposes candidates for office at any level of government and acts as a respected neutral party in political events such as candidate debates. Some of its members also serve as election officials.

Election Officials

Every polling place in the United States relies on election officials to ensure fair, orderly voting, protect the rights of voters, and enforce voting laws and regulations. Requirements for serving as an election official vary from state to state, but all require officials to be registered voters. States also prohibit candidates seeking office, as well as members of the candidates' families, from serving as election officials.

Election officials must undergo training before Election Day to become familiar with both the procedures and the machinery for voting. They learn how to assist voters without influencing, interfering with, or intruding upon the right to vote freely and secretly. Above all, election officials must be impartial. They cannot promote a specific candidate and cannot wear or display any items that advertise a candidate or a political party.

On November 8, [2006] the streamers will be down, the signs removed, and all the related trappings of a spirited campaign season packed away, as the volunteers return to their usual routines and their newly elected leaders get on with the business of governance. And, in offices scattered across the nation, the planning will begin for the 2008 elections.

4

Outsourced Activism Has Limited Impact on Political Campaigns

Dana R. Fisher

Dana R. Fisher is an associate professor of sociology at Columbia University and the author of Activism Inc.: How the Outsourcing of Grassroots Campaigns Is Strangling Progressive Politics in America.

Modern door-to-door activism traces its roots to the early 1970s and has evolved into a commonly used tactic by political parties and interest groups that employ professional canvassers. Unfortunately, there are a range of problems with this type of activism. Professionals usually do not have the same zeal or passion for topics as volunteers and it is not unusual to have paid canvassers work for both sides of an issue. The political left, including the Democratic Party, most commonly uses outsourced activism, but the Republicans demonstrated in the 2004 election that grassroots initiatives can be more effective. Nonetheless, the trend is for increased paid activism.

You've seen them before. The crunchy-looking college-aged twentysomethings who knock at your door on summer evenings or stand on street corners across the country. Dressed in the T-shirts of progressive organizations like Save the Children or the Sierra Club, clipboards in hand they step into your path, smile, and make eye contact: "Hey there, how's it going? Do you have a minute?"

Grassroots Outreach

This type of grassroots outreach was born on May 27, 1971, when Marc Anderson, a former encyclopedia salesman, decided to combine his door-to-door sales knowledge with the political experience he gained volunteering for a local candidate's campaign. Harvard law student and self-described "Nader's Raider" [after activist Ralph Nadar] David Zwick became intrigued by Anderson's efforts while he was trying to fund his newly formed group Clean Water Action. Learning the technique from Anderson, Zwick used issue-based canvassing to develop and sustain his work, which is now supported by 700,000 citizen members around the country. Zwick notes that all of the issue-based groups that have canvassed in the past 30-plus years can be traced back to Anderson's work, either via his direct management or through people he trained spinning off to run canvasses for other groups: "Virtually all today are either imitators or direct descendants."

During the 1990s, as the funding for progressive causes waned, many national progressive groups were forced to tighten their belts and close their local field offices. Like corporations that hire workers in India to run their call centers, the canvassing, phone banking, and direct mail outreach that sustains the fundraising and membership base of progressive organizations and campaigns in America were outsourced to national groups that emerged to fill the gap on the left. As word spread of this efficient and cost-effective way to develop and maintain a grassroots base, national groups that had never worked at the grassroots level also decided to outsource. Today, progressive groups have only to sign up with an intermediary organization and trained canvassers will go door-to-door or work the sidewalk traffic on their behalf, dressed in the group's T-shirt and armed with pitches that work.

The system is indeed more efficient. Unfortunately, this type of outsourced politics increases the distance between members and the progressive national groups that claim to represent them and has proven no match for the kind of political institutions on the right that are locally rooted and turn citizens into engaged activists.

The Fund for Public Interest Research

One of the largest of the progressive grassroots clearinghouses is the Fund for Public Interest Research, which currently runs campaigns from numerous progressive groups simultaneously. In summer 2003, for example, the Fund ran campaigns for more than fifteen organizations around the United States, including the Sierra Club, the Human Rights Campaign, Save the Children, and Greenpeace. Their model of grassroots politics is very successful at recruiting members and raising funds. Sally Green Heaven, the Deputy Field Director of the Human Rights Campaign (HRC), reported that their membership has grown from 200,000 to 600,000 members since the group started outsourcing to the Fund in the late 1990s. According to John Passacantando, the Executive Director of Greenpeace USA: "[The Fund] helped us build our new financial base. It gave us a new base and it paid approximately 25 percent of our yearly income from monthly electronic donations, which is huge."

Canvassers at the Fund are expected to bounce from one campaign to another. In the words of HRC president Joe Solmonese, "The person who is out standing on the street corner trying to sign you up to join HRC, they honestly, like the next day, might be doing the same thing for [a different organization]." As a result of their short shelf lives and having to juggle multiple campaigns, most canvassers do not become particularly committed to the cause. (Turnover is notoriously high.)

Beyond raising money, it is unclear how effective canvassers can be at building grassroots support when they have such limited knowledge of and passion for the campaigns. One long-term canvasser I met in Portland spoke to me just before canvassing on behalf of Save the Children. When I asked him about the group, he replied: "Yeah I don't know too much. You probably know as much as I do."

Outsourced Politics

This system has become so regimented and widespread that another long-term canvasser who worked out of the Fund's Atlanta office actually called it a "monopoly on political organizing" for the left. In fact, this type of outsourced politics maintains the grassroots base for approximately 25 percent of the largest left-leaning membership organizations in the United States. (This number is calculated based on the members of the progressive advocacy group coalition America Votes who outsource their canvassing.) In 2004 this type of political outsourcing expanded to electoral politics. During the presidential election, the Democratic National Committee hired a for-profit spin-off of the Fund to extend its political base. As a result, canvassers dressed in DNC T-shirts stood on sidewalks around the country raising funds for the Democratic Party. Josh Wachs, the Executive Director of the DNC during the 2004 election, reflected on the success of this outsourced canvassing for the Party: "We created hundreds of thousands of new grassroots donors, 90-some percent of which were new to the party. There were 700,000 new donors who were created through [it], which is really an incredible amount."

> [P]rogressive causes and progressive candidates have been losing out to conservative issues and candidates who use a very different model of organization.

This type of outsourced politics is widespread in electoral campaigns on the left. According to Karen Hicks, who worked as the National Field Director for the Democratic Party in 2004 after running Howard Dean's presidential campaign for the state of New Hampshire: "The trend within the Democratic Party has really been to outsource contact with voters to paid vendors and direct mail firms [as well as] hiring people just to contact voters because it's a shortcut. It's a more reliable way to do it."

Although she recognized the efficiency of outsourcing grassroots politics, Hicks also noted that canvassing does not foster long-term dedication and commitment or develop much local infrastructure: "At the end of the campaign, you're left with nothing, basically, because all those canvassers walk out the door. It's not a job that most people do time and time again." So the organizations get members and money out of canvassers, and most of the canvassers go back to their schools or jobs, or move on to an entirely different campaign when its over. As a result, this type of outsourced politics leaves the grassroots base on the left disconnected and disorganized.

Indeed, progressive causes and progressive candidates have been losing out to conservative issues and candidates who use a very different model of organization. In contrast to the outsourced politics of the left, political groups on the right work through pre-existing civic associations formed by churches and other locally grounded networks to create lasting connections with its political base. Adopting more and more of the social conservative platform originally developed by the Christian Coalition, Republicans are able to tap into the extensive network of local groups that the Coalition developed since its creation in the late 1980s.

Republican Efforts

In the 2004 presidential election, the Bush-Cheney campaign instituted a strategy designed to exploit such local connections. The Republican Party's "72-hour Plan" was designed to get out the Republican vote by taking advantage of these ever-expanding networks of conservative Americans. Originally conceived to provide a blueprint for the final 72 hours of a campaign, its goal was to recruit Bush supporters—both young and old—through a complex network of local volunteers contacting Republican and Republican-leaning voters. The National Conservative Coalitions' Director for the Bush campaign, Gary Marx, stated that the Plan mobilized economic and social conservatives through each individual's "sphere of influence." Volunteers who were recruited through their friends and neighbors were taught how to implement the 72-hour Plan in their communities through trainings and the campaign's sophisticated web site.

While the Republicans rallied local networks of conservatives to work on the Bush campaign, the Democrats relied on paid professionals and imported volunteers from blue states to canvass and work for them to turn out the vote on Election Day. Although the Democrats mobilized more people than ever before with the help of 527 political groups like America Coming Together, the outcome of the 2004 election speaks for itself: having non-local people go door-to-door with clipboards is not as effective as mobilizing locals *already* living in those neighborhoods to speak with their friends and neighbors. Laurie Moskowitz, a political consultant who directed the DNC's field effort for the Gore campaign in 2000 and worked on the grassroots mobilization of progressive Americans during the 2004 campaign through an independent firm, explains: "The Republicans built a system that was based on personal connections over time [they] had the time and energy invested in it, and the resources [with the 72-hour Plan] you had your ten people based on that personal connection. At the end of the day, we just were trying to make contacts."

The Dangers of Outsourcing

In recent years, there has been some recognition of the dangers of outsourcing progressive politics. John Passacantando pointed out that canvassing used to be a major entry point for activists to get involved with his organization, but after outsourcing to the Fund, Greenpeace could no longer mobilize canvassers to participate in political actions. After comprehending the need to combine their fundraising with their activism in a more meaningful way, and noting the fact that the members who signed up through their outsourced canvass did not stay on very long, Greenpeace became one of the only national organizations to buck the outsourcing trend. As of December 2004, Greenpeace was no longer outsourcing its grassroots outreach. Instead, it is experimenting with running its own local campaigns.

Beyond this one environmental group, however, the trend continues. As a result of this political shortcut, the distance between progressive Americans and the national groups and political candidates that purport to represent them is growing. More importantly, progressive candidates and progressive issues keep losing to conservative counterparts that have invested the time and the money to develop real local ties to Americans.

5

Internet Activism Has
Revolutionized Politics

Laura D'Amelio

Laura D'Amelio is a journalist with a master's degree in Environmental Communications and Journalism who writes about ecological and conservation issues.

Environmental activists are increasingly using the Internet as a means to spread their message and to coordinate efforts. The Web has made it easier to communicate with fellow activists and to organize grassroots efforts on specific initiatives. The Internet has been especially beneficial to rural and remote environmentalists by providing them the means to draw attention to local issues and gain support from outside of their community. Newer technologies also allow groups to disseminate information more quickly and for less money. However, the Internet should be seen as one of many tools, and it works best when used in conjunction with more traditional activist strategies.

In 1971, early Greenpeacers set out with long-haired, steely determination in a worn-out boat towards Amchitka, Alaska, to oppose nuclear testing. The famous voyage brought international attention to environmental issues. Told and retold over the years, the lyrical prose used to describe the actions of the first Greenpeace activists seems poetic and inspiring to any environmental campaigner.

The Internet and Environmental Activism

But these days, the environmental movement's biggest ruckus comes from the collective clicking of a mouse or tapping of a

Laura D'Amelio, "Wired for Action," *Alternatives Journal*, vol. 31, Spring 2005, pp. 14–15. Reproduced by permission of the author.

keyboard. Organizations and campaigns of all sizes have turned to the Internet to win fast support for their causes.

Activism has never been easier. Type your name at the end of a pre-formed letter and click the send button. In the span of half an hour you can protest pollution legislation in Ontario, bear bile farming in China, grizzly bear hunting in [British Columbia], imprisonment of journalists in Eritrea or genetically modified crops in Paraguay. Then ask the Colombian government to negotiate with indigenous peoples affected by a proposed hydroelectric dam, all before your morning fair-trade coffee.

Action alerts let supporters know through email when their help is needed, e-newsletters keep them up to date, and chat rooms give way to virtual organizational meetings. To adopt the word used frequently to refer to this new breed of Internet crusader, "cyberactivists" are responding in the thousands.

The Greenpeace Example

Greenpeace, pioneering again, offers a site dedicated solely to cyberactivism tools such as petitions and letter writing. Website visitors can also download action kits, letting them take campaigns to the streets with ready-made posters and leaflets.

What we tried to do is capitalize on the viral nature of the Internet . . . [word] spreads very fast. . .

The Internet can help the average citizen to take the reins, starting small-scale campaigns in response to local issues. In New Brunswick, [Canada], residents are waging a cyberbattle against Bennett Environmental Inc.'s plans to operate a soil incinerator in Belledune designed to treat soils contaminated with [pollutants such as] PCBs, PCPs, pesticides and chlorinated organic compounds.

Environmental Studies major Allain Frigault, with his web developer brother Robert, launched their website, Stop Bennett Environmental Inc., in February of 2004.

"Our purpose was to serve as a community of interest around an environmental cause, to promote awareness and incite action," says Frigault. "We felt that people weren't given a chance to get involved. It wasn't that people didn't care, it's just that they had no way to voice their opinions."

Capitalizing on the Internet

This website is an addition to many offline organizations and petitions already addressing this issue. Still, stopbennett.com boasts over 1400 unique visitors per month and more than 1200 other websites are linked to it. Seventy percent of the site's visitors sign the petition, garnering over 10,000 signatures to date. Petitioners from France and South Korea, mostly Canadians living abroad, have now joined a list of high profile visitors to the site which includes media outlets and federal governmental departments.

This technology lets remote activists communicate new happenings, and helps average citizens document local environmental issues.

"What we tried to do is capitalize on the viral nature of the Internet," Frigault says. "Word spreads very fast, so we encouraged visitors to tell their friends about the petition and this site. This is how we built an audience."

This is also how coalitions and networks are built. One of the most dynamic aspects of the Internet is its built-in capacity for linking groups and causes. Groups can readily create alliances and benefit from the support of every group's members for campaigns and events.

It's that type of collaboration that Rex Turgano hopes will emerge from his site, thegreenpages.ca. The searchable directory supplies information about environmental issues across Canada, by province, subject and upcoming events.

Turgano continuously refreshes the site to keep visitors coming back. He recently added an "action alert" section and a blog to keep users updated. It seems to be working—there were close to 200,000 visits to the site in 2004. Blogs, short for weblogs, are online personal diaries. This technology lets remote activists communicate new happenings, and helps average citizens document local environmental issues. Internet gurus and academics alike point to blogs as a potent tool for environmental advocacy.

That is, of course, if their words can result in offline actions. Knowing the technology and having a website does not automatically translate into success.

Communicopia.net

Communicopia.net is an 11-year-old online communications company that helps organizations use the Internet to connect with and engage their audiences. President Jason Mogus emphasizes, "It's not just the technology—everyone's got an email newsletter these days. It's how you apply it, whether you can make it successful and engaging. This is a way for organizations to broaden their base and reach people."

He notes his company's work with the BC Chapter of the Sierra Club. A revamped website and new tools that help supporters take action are matched with an e-newsletter, *SIERRA life*, that engages readers.

"I guess the old formula was to only contact people when you had something you wanted them to take action on," says Taylor Bachrach, communications director of the Sierra Club's BC chapter. "So we are trying to broaden our scope of communications by including environmental lifestyle information with tips on ecology and smart consumerism."

Bachrach says the tactic has been working. Subscription to the newsletter, which also lets readers know about issues and campaigns, has increased from 800 to 2,500 subscribers in just over a year.

But Internet approaches cannot survive alone, says Mogus. "It always has to be integrated into your offline communications—the two reinforce each other and help organizations use each medium to their best advantage."

Benefits of Internet Campaigns

Internet strategies bring a host of benefits to environmental campaigns. Communications are more effective and less costly. Instead of "broadcasting" your message through traditional media to a general audience, the Net allows for "narrowcasting," targeting a specific audience of supporters. The ease with which visitors can find background information and take action also helps drum up extra support for a cause. By focusing on the quality of the site and constantly adding features, web campaigners keep visitors coming back.

But every technology has its downside. The Net's accessibility and pervasiveness have many using it as a platform. "There are so many organizations and we are always competing for funding and support and new members," says Turgano. "Some have overlapping initiatives and it's a double-edged sword. Their site helps them get their information out, but for the consumer, it's a lot of stuff to go through."

According to Mogus, "There are two sides to that story. If you're really strong in your niche, then people will find you." "But," he adds, "for the general organizations that want to reach the general public, unfortunately, there are still way too many environmental groups out there. Personally, I think that's ultimately not serving the needs of the movement."

Spam and Privacy Issues

Concerns over privacy and email spam continue to trouble the online strategy. As does the "digital divide." The technologically advanced and rich North undeniably benefits from a wired world. Despite the wealth of Northern nations, computer access is not evenly distributed. And with little or no access to this resource in the South, the disparity is even more severe, where the ability to share information and organize movements is much needed but greatly hindered.

While environmental consciousness has been slowly growing in today's society, it remains to be seen if the Internet can create a thrust of interest and action that harkens back to the early days of Greenpeace voyages.

A website is, after all, ineffectual unless an interested person chooses to visit it. "The online stuff is only one component of doing grassroots works," says Bachrach. "Because the most important thing is being in personal contact with your members through events, getting out on the street and talking to people."

6

The Internet Has Revolutionized Political Campaigns

Michael Cornfield

Michael Cornfield is the director of Research for the Democracy Online Project and an adjunct professor at George Washington University.

Democratic presidential candidate Howard Dean effectively used the Internet to initially outpace his rivals in fundraising and campaign momentum. Dean's campaign demonstrated that the Web and the Internet were potentially powerful tools in a political effort. Professional campaign workers were slow to adapt to the new technology and incorporate it into an integrated approach that combined old and new styles. Instead, the true potential of the Internet is only just beginning to be realized.

The news in presidential politics early in the summer of 2003 caught many people by surprise. The leading candidate for the 2004 Democratic presidential nomination was an obscure former governor from a tiny state with a reputation for offbeat politics, a man with no personal fortune to spend and no organized or identity-based constituency to count on as a base of support. Howard Dean was nevertheless anointed by the national news media as a serious contender. Unlike Jimmy Carter, a candidate with a similarly slender political base, Dean had not prevailed in the Iowa caucuses to make the covers of *Time, Newsweek,* and *U.S. News & World Report.* That first vote in the race for convention delegates was still

Michael Cornfield, *Politics Moves Online: Campaigning and the Internet.* New York: The Century Foundation Press, 2004. Reproduced by permission.

half a year away. Instead, Dean had finished ahead of his competitors in the "MoveOn.org primary" and "the money primary." Tens of thousands of his supporters were congregating at monthly "Meetups," and conversing in "discussion groups" and "blogs." Over a quarter of a million people had given the Dean campaign their "e-mail" addresses.

The Internet and Political Campaigns

Blogs? MoveOn.org? As recently as a decade ago, these achievements would have struck even the most sophisticated observers of the race for the presidency as political science fiction. What they represent, instead, is the flowering of campaigning on the Internet. . . .

The Dean phenomenon cannot be fully appreciated without a somewhat arbitrary yet necessary distinction between "the Net" and "the Web." In common parlance, the two phrases are interchangeable. Many people also use the term "Web site" as a synonym for a campaign presence on the Internet. Yet the Dean campaign Web site, www.deanforamerica.com, provides the slightest of clues to the campaign's success. It has the same format and kinds of information as the Web sites for Dean's competitors and, indeed, most campaign Web sites at the statewide or federal levels. But there is more to the Net than just the Web, let alone a particular Web site.

[T]he ease with which Internet users flit from product to product, and from page to page within a product, suggests that understanding communications in this medium requires a reorientation.

Focusing on a single Web site reflects a mass communications mentality oriented to the sequential consumption of individual media products. A book is a media product read from cover to cover; a television show is watched from start to finish; advertisements placed in a profusion of places and formats entice people to read the book and watch the show. Beginning, middle, end, go to the next one; beginning, middle, end, go to the next one: for people over thirty, this is a mass media consumption rhythm inculcated since early childhood. A newspaper, magazine, CD, or DVD comes closer to the Net/Web experience. These mass media products have numbered pages or segments that indicate a main sequence to be followed, but their modular structure permits consumption out of sequence.

In contrast, the ease with which Internet users flit from product to product, and from page to page within a product, suggests that understanding communications in this medium requires a reorientation. One must focus on the connections as much as the contents. The Internet, or Net, is an electronic platform for establishing social connections. Campaigns turn to the Net and the myriad of distribution channels, interactive forums, and message formats it houses—Web sites, yes, but also e-mail, instant messaging, discussion groups, blogs (a sort of diary that permits others to comment), pop-up advertisements, searchable databases, and so forth—in order to win an election. The more voters a campaign establishes connections with, the better it will fare. More important, in these early years of online campaigning, the more activists a campaign ensnares in its network-on-the-Net, the more money and volunteer hours it will collect, and the more voters it will be able to reach through mass media and physical contacts.

Deanforamerica.com

Like most campaign Web sites, Deanforamerica.com contains an assortment of promotional material, digital versions of the stuff that has lain on candidate display tables for decades. The first paragraphs of news releases and position papers run down the center column of the home page. Biographical material about the candidate and photographs from the campaign trail may be accessed from the left-hand column, while the right-hand column features sign-up boxes for petitions, volunteer work, contributions, and voter registration, along with a link to the online store where buttons and bumper-stickers may be purchased. None of this would startle the political sophisticate from the recent past. And none of it would knock an online campaign specialist, or dot-pol, for a loop. A dot-pol would regard much of Deanforamerica.com's contents as "brochureware," yesterday's formats transposed to today's new medium, vaudeville skits on television.

For an appreciation of the political power that the Dean campaign has extracted from its Internet presence, one must be alert to the structural significance of a quartet of simulated file folder tabs running along the top of the Deanforamerica-.com home page. "Contribute" opens a virtual door to electronic donations, either on a one-time basis or through an installment plan that deducts a designated amount from a credit card account every month until the donor has reached the legal maximum. "Get Local" brings the site visitor to a database of upcoming campaign events, searchable within one hundred or the visitor's choice of miles from any zip code in the nation. This tab also features a toolkit to help volunteers plan events and a link to MeetUp.com, a company that uses the Internet to arrange monthly gatherings of people with common interests at coffeehouses, restaurants, and other public locales.

DeanLink

"DeanLink" provides a means for individuals to put together their own networks through e-mail, instant messaging, and dedicated pages on the Dean Web site. An imitation of Friendster, a commercial online dating service, DeanLink relies on the desire for social contact as a springboard to campaign involvement. Access is screened and monitored through password-entry software. The preeminent DeanLinker as of October 12, 2003, was Jonathan Kriess-Tomkins of Sitka, Alaska. The Web page about him provided links to pages about the 447 persons linked to the Dean campaign through him, a list of his interests, a link to his personal home page, and a photograph of him holding an ice-cream cone. (Jonathan is fourteen years old.)

[T]he Dean campaign assembled by far the biggest and most active online campaign network.

"Official Blog" leads to blogforamerica.com, a parallel Web site to that of the campaign. The middle column contains diary entries from a handful of Dean campaign managers in reverse chronological order; the top entry is usually no more than a few hours old. A blog reader can send any entry to a friend, trace it back through preceding entries to which it is intimately related, or follow it through to comments posted by other readers. In this way, visitors to blogforamerica.com pick up threads of monologues and conversations, as though they were wandering through a campaign headquarters. The right column reprises calls to action posted on the regular campaign Web site and catalogs the blog entries by the time and day they appeared and by category. The left column consists of hundreds of links to Dean-related activity elsewhere on the Web, mostly run by supporters with no official ties to the campaign. Deanybopper clips articles from major newspapers. The Dean Defense Forces call talk shows and write editors to correct what they perceive as unfair coverage. Switch To Dean, imitating an advertising campaign of Apple Computer, collects and displays homemade Web videos with testimonials from erstwhile supporters of other candidates who have now committed to Dean. The Dean Corps puts volunteers to work in local communities in Iowa, cleaning up rivers and collecting supplies for schools and food banks.

Other campaigns have established similar features. But the Dean campaign has assembled by far the biggest and most active online campaign network. On October 15, 2003, according to the campaign, there were 466,884 people on the e-mail list, 123,331 had signed up to attend a Meetup, 78,330 had attended at least one of 6,177 events organized through the Get Local feature, and 168,000 had donated an average of $73.69 in the July–September 2003 quarter for a total of $14.8 million. That set a record for quarterly fund-raising by a Democratic presidential candidate, and brought the total raised in 2003 to $25.3 million. (In the same third quarter, the Bush re-election campaign raised $49.5 million and touted the 145,000 contributions of less than $200.)

The average amount of a Dean donation was as remarkable a tribute to the strength of his support network as the amount the campaign raised. According to the Campaign Finance Institute, 70 percent of all individual donations to major-party presidential candidates in the first nine months of 2003 came in contributions of $1,000 or more. The comparable statistic for 1999 was 67 percent. But Dean raised 55 percent of his millions in donations of $200 or less. The Dean network also has contributed tactical intelligence. The campaign took the advice of a supporter in deciding to solicit handwritten letters from MeetUp attendees to uncommitted voters in Iowa and New Hampshire. . . .

The Impact of Dean

Dean used his online network to help him win at two new stops on the campaign trail, which also would not be conceivable without the Internet. The MoveOn.org primary was a straw poll staged by an online activist group. . . . Dean won 139,360 votes, 44 percent of the total; more significant, he reaped 54,730 volunteer pledges, 49,132 financial pledges, and 77,192 additions to the campaign e-mail list. The money primary, . . . is a veritable straw poll created by a confluence of online activities by political campaigns, journalists, and the Federal Election Commission. . . .

The Web and Professional Campaigning

Those campaigners with a special interest in adapting the Internet to their work will be referred to as "dot-pols"; they are change agents who constitute a critical subset of the campaigning community. Online and off-line, campaigners initiate the bulk of political action in the public square, which elicits reactions from journalists, citizens, and policymakers. Policymakers are, of course, often the same people who campaign. But the two modes of operation are different and create dilemmas of priority. Whereas policymakers seek above all to govern, that is, to steer the ship of state on the basis of legal authority, collaborative negotiations, and deliberative dialogue, the primary objective of campaigners is to win an upcoming vote by an electorate, legislative, or other decisionmaking body.

Since the late 1960s, campaigning has been increasingly dominated by a blend of marketing and military techniques known as the "professional" style. The professional campaign is by now distinctive and pervasive enough to be disparaged abroad as the "American" campaign. Its communicative core consists of for-hire specialists directing politicians in the repetition of carefully designed statements, or messages, to carefully specified audiences, or targets. The conventional channels for targeted messages are broadcast and cable television (the locus of the "air war"); rally sites, meeting halls, mall entrances, and residential doorsteps (the "ground war"); and radio, telephone, bulk or "direct" mail, and graphic displays (not called the "war at sea," but no less essential for lacking a metaphorically apt nickname).

Professional campaigners take an elaborate approach to political communication, known as message development. A message is the central rationale and motivation the public must accept in order for it to act as the campaign desires. It may be thought of as the words that complete the sentence that begins, "Vote for us because. . . ." Because it's the economy, stupid. Because we have a Contract with America. Because we'll build a bridge to the twenty-first century. Because if the glove don't fit, you must acquit. Because we are compassionate conservatives. Campaign professionals ask clients what they want and guide them in the articulation of a message that will win them the support they need to prevail with a decisionmaking body. Message development is not rocket science, but it is not as obvious as the best practitioners make it look, for it is embedded at every stage—research, creation, testing, and release—in complex, expensive, and customized uses of technology.

Professional Activists

The consultants and staffers who direct the production and distribution of campaign communication are preponderantly white, male, young, well educated, and ideologically moderate. They love the all-consuming, historically and ideologically tinged competition of politics, so much so that the most successful ones forgo or curtail steadier, more lucrative jobs in public relations and advertising, which campaigning resembles in many respects. There are fundamental differences though between selling candidates and selling cars. A campaigner's "products" need far more than market share to be considered successful, and they are not available for sale every day. The product features of politics consist of issue positions and character traits, which are harder to define than a commercial good. Like the car sellers, however, the basis of the campaigners' power resides in the perception among their clients that they possess expertise in how to use communications technologies in ambiguous and often volatile situations.

These political clients fall into two basic categories, according to their electoral or policy orientation. In the former, more visible category, campaign professionals are hired by candidates for office and the political parties that nominate and funnel money to them. In the latter, more stable category, corporations, interest groups, trade associations, unions, and coalitions thereof contract with campaign professionals to help them win a decision before a government body and, more generally, to "manage issues," that is, maintain a good public image with respect to affairs in which they have a stake. Issue management occurs every day of every year and sometimes consists of forestalling votes instead of trying to win them. So it comes as no surprise to learn which campaign category is larger: In 2000, approximately $4 billion was spent on electoral campaigns in the United States, $3 billion of it at the national level. The policy campaign market that year was estimated at $35 billion. These figures may seem large. Campaign finance reformers often make them seem so. But while the business of campaigning rose sharply during the 1990s, it represents a mere 1–2 percent of the polling, advertising, telemarketing, and public relations markets.

The Internet presented professional campaigners with a subtle and sizable challenge.

Campaigners are not full professionals, like doctors, lawyers, and architects. They do not need a license, verified mastery of a codified body of knowledge, and pledged fealty to a code of ethics in order to sell their services. Rather, like journalists, campaigners are semiprofessionals, in that they are imbued with a sense of public service that complicates and can even override their business commitments to their clients. It runs against the popular stereotype to speak of campaign professionals as political idealists. But very few of them will work for very long on behalf of clients who do not share their dreams for American politics. It is an unspoken and nearly unbreakable rule in the vocation that Democrats work for Democratic clients and Republicans for Republican clients. Many policy consulting firms are bipartisan ventures, with a star from each party on the nameplate to maximize the client list without violating the precept.

Challenges of the Internet

The Internet presented professional campaigners with a subtle and sizable challenge. At first glance, the new communications technology resembled many of the media channels and devices that campaigners used to win votes and earn a living. A campaign Web site was like the reception area of a headquarters, a place for brochures and other publicity materials. The rest of the Web was analogous to a library in one sense, and to a grid of streets and highways in another: the places where one did research and put up billboards. E-mail was a fabulous melding of the telephone, fax, and postal service. Instant or text messaging could be understood as enhanced pagers. And computerized databases corresponded to the file cabinets in the back of the headquarters.

But there the analogies ended. Each of these components of the Internet were intimately connected through the electronic network. Each could be used by many persons at every minute of the day from every spot on earth, some accessing the system according to plan but some randomly, some anonymously, and some surreptitiously. Messages could move at the speed of light, and they could also stay within reach for years. Connection lines, traffic patterns, and message components could all be analyzed and automatically improved by computer programs. And every day, it seemed, a better version of one aspect of the technology hit the market, making it a constant effort to stay on the cutting edge and, more important, to stay connected to as many people as possible.

The arrival of the Internet in American society thus meant several things at once to the professional politicking community. It was a threat to business as usual, an opportunity for new firms and new divisions of established firms, an unknown factor in an already complicated communications milieu, and an object of fashionable curiosity.

7

Student Activism Has Dramatically Affected American Politics

Glenn Omatsu

Glenn Omatsu teaches courses in service learning and Asian-American studies at the University of California, Northside, and is the coeditor of the book Asian Americans: The Movement and the Moment.

The growing gap between the prosperous and the less fortunate in the world necessitates greater activism among students, especially those in the United States. American student activists have had tremendous success in influencing policy at the national, state and local levels. They have fundamentally altered the nature and curriculum of higher education and drawn attention to issues of inequality around the world. Student activists are most successful when they build coalitions with other groups to enact "social change and transformation" within societies. Finally, activism needs to be intertwined with education and individuals must lead the effort to change societies and cultures, beginning at the local level.

Today, the world is in great turmoil. Not only do we see war and destruction, but we also see growing poverty and hunger, the emergence of new slavery, and the ravaging of our ecosystem. Some have defined the modern world not in terms of technological advances but in terms of the growing gap be-

Glenn Omatsu, *Student Activism Resource Handbook.* April 2002, pp. 1–9. Reproduced by permission of the author.

tween "haves" and "have nots." This division of the world's population is not simply economic but also social and political—i.e., a separation of world populations between those with basic human rights and those without. In fact, it is probably more accurate to describe today's world not as a division between "haves" and "have nots" but rather between "haves" and "disposable people." Today's "disposable people" are those who toil for pennies a day in sweatshops for global corporations, those who are kidnapped and trafficked in modern-day slavery, and those without access to basic necessities such as fresh drinking water.

Student Activism

Historically, in times of crisis, student activism has been a crucial force for social change. Students around the world have been at the forefront of movements to promote democracy and human rights. Student movements have toppled powerful dictatorships and military juntas. Student movements have ended wars. And student activism has often served as the conscience for nations, reminding people in times of turmoil of the founding ideals of their countries and the aspirations of all people for justice, dignity, and equality. Thus, it comes as no surprise that the world's most repressive governments jail and often murder student activists, close down college campuses during times of crisis, and enforce strict guidelines about what can and cannot be taught in school systems. Those in power understand the significance of student movements—often more so than student activists themselves.

In the California State University system, student activism has transformed our campuses and surrounding communities. At San Francisco State University in 1968–69, students went out on strike in order to gain classes and departments in Ethnic Studies. Their strike lasting six months stands as the longest student strike in U.S. history. At California State University, Northridge, in the late 1960s, student activists mobilized to create several important institutions that are a vibrant part of our campus today: the Ethnic Studies departments and the Educational Opportunity Program (EOP). Many of the original ideas advanced by student activists for transforming education at CSUN have now become embraced throughout the CSU system. Some of these ideas—which at one time were viewed as controversial and radical—are service-learning, interdisciplinary instruction, student advisement, student tutorial services provided by peer mentors, and transitional summer programs for entering freshmen.

The Power of Student Activism

How do student movements become so powerful? Student movements gain power not because they are composed of militant and dedicated students. Student movements draw their power through the formation of strategic alliances with other sectors of society facing oppression, such as immigrants, workers, racial minorities, women, and peasants and other dispossessed peoples in the countryside. By joining in solidarity with others, student movements gain the power necessary to transform society.

Thus, student activism is about social change and transformation.

In order to form alliances with other sectors of society, students must educate themselves and others about issues facing these sectors. Thus, student activism is as much about educating and organizing as about engaging in actions such as participating in rallies and marches. Or more accurately, becoming an activist requires a new understanding about the relationship between educating, organizing, and acting. Unlike the traditional academic approach that separates knowing the world from interacting with it, activism requires rethinking the relationship between thinking and doing. "Praxis" is the term that captures this new understanding. Praxis connects knowing and doing, theory and practice. Only in academia are knowing and doing regarded as separate things; in reality, knowing and doing are parts of the same process. In the course of everyday life, we are always simultaneously thinking and acting, and gaining wisdom and maturity is based on training ourselves to reflect constantly about our actions and to carry out actions based on an understanding of consequences and responsibilities. Becoming an activist helps each person become conscious of their role as an agent of historical and social change.

Activism is essentially about raising awareness and promoting education to help liberate and empower our communities.

Social Change and Transformation

Thus, student activism is about social change and transformation. But is the focus of activists only on changing the institutions of society? No, it is not! Changing society must be done in tandem with changing oneself. Otherwise, activists within their own movements and in the new social institutions they create will simply end up replicating the same relationships of oppression that they are fighting. Nor can we wait until later— "after the revolution," after the creation of new institutions, or after "we have gotten into power"—to address serious problems like racism, sexism, homophobia, etc. that plague human relationships. These issues must be addressed as part of our ongoing struggles to change the world. In other words, activism must be viewed as engaging in both social change and personal transformation simultaneously. We cannot change injustices in the world without also confronting and overcoming injustices in our own practices.

For student activists in universities, personal transformation requires grappling with the question of privileges that they have as students. In all societies around the world, students who attend universities are a relatively privileged segment. After all, having the time and resources to acquire knowledge and to study and think critically about issues are, unfortunately, privileges in the world today. Privileged status brings a choice: how will a person use these privileges? Will the privileges be used to advance oneself economically and socially, even if it means ignoring oppression and destruction all around and perhaps even helping to perpetuate these conditions? Or will a person use privileges to confront and eliminate the conditions of oppression and destruction? Student activists are those who have seriously pondered these questions and have consciously decided to use their resources, time, and talents to confront social problems. . . .

Activism and Education

Activism is essentially about raising awareness and promoting education to help liberate and empower our communities. Awareness and education open people to new ways of thinking and new ways of looking at the world around them. New ways of thinking enable people to confront and solve problems in different ways.

What is needed in the current period is a new kind of education—an education for our liberation. On the one hand, this requires activists to expand the content of education by bringing to the forefront issues of globalization, corporate accountability, human rights, racism and sexism, and a host of other topics to help people understand the world.

But developing an education for our liberation goes beyond questions of content. It also requires activists to adopt a new approach to education—an approach that sees education as a process linked to organizing and centered on human interactions. This new approach to education is related to latest insights coming from cognitive scientists and brain-based educational research as well as the wisdom passed down to us by indigenous peoples around the world.

Activism and Social Learning

Humans are essentially social beings. According to the latest research focusing on learning and the human brain, the vast majority of people learn through social interactions. In many ways, the latest scientific information about human learning validates the approach to education used for centuries in indigenous peoples' cultures emphasizing mentoring relationships between children and elders, learning by doing, and a learning environment marked by rich, intergenerational interactions. In contrast, the existing model of instruction used in most American schools stresses individual learning through lectures and standardized tests, and largely isolates children from "elders" of the community. This standard model of education probably hinders learning for most children. More importantly, it serves as an institution for social control and perpetuation of current hierarchies of power.

The Importance of Young Activists

Thus, in this period, conceptualizing and implementing a new approach to education—an education for our liberation—is very difficult for activists. It is difficult because it requires activists to address questions of educational content currently outside the scope of today's education system. And it is even more difficult because it requires activists to retrieve and recreate a new approach to education that is contrary to the existing approach.

In this critical period in world history, we need more people—especially youth—to take up the challenge of becoming activist-educators in our communities. Educate to Liberate!

Political Organizing

Ideas for social change come from individuals—or, more accurately, they come from individuals through discussions with others. Individuals can turn ideas into action, but truly effective action emerges from collective efforts involving large numbers of people at the grassroots level. In other words, social change hinges on the ability of individual activists to organize with others collectively. This requires not only the reaching of common goals and a common understanding of issues but also grasping the importance of forging new human relationships based on mutual respect and solidarity. Thus, effective activists are essentially political organizers who have devoted time to keenly develop skills in bringing people together through community education and promoting interrelationships based on respect and solidarity. . . .

It is fairly common in all grassroots political movements to hear some activists complain about apathy in their community.

Strategies for political change are strategies for political organizing. Although each political situation is unique and must be appreciated for its uniqueness, all organizing strategies share several things in common. First, they help people to analyze power relations in society and provide insights into how unequal relations can be changed. Second, they focus on uniting all who can be united around common goals and new human values. Third, they help people to connect specific political issues with broader issues; in other words, they enable people to understand the interconnections and interrelatedness between issues. Fourth, they emphasize the active involvement of people in the decisions that affect their lives; in other words, they enable people to discover the power within themselves to change their lives and to change society. In short, social change is not made by individual activists who devise strategies for manipulating or acting upon others. Social change occurs when activists through interactions with others enable people collectively to find the power within themselves to become active agents making their own history.

Where do organizing strategies come from? Do they emerge fully developed from the minds of geniuses? Are they found in books (or, today, on websites) of experienced activists? No! Organizing strategies develop from intense and ongoing discussions at the grassroots level among people striving to reach a common understanding of critical issues facing them and seeking to create a path for their own liberation. There are no magical shortcuts in this often difficult process, although people can draw from the accumulated wisdom of past generations and contemporaries around the globe involved in similar movements for social change.

It is fairly common in all grassroots political movements to hear some activists complain about apathy in their community. "The people just aren't interested in fighting for justice. They don't care. They don't want to become involved." Remarks like these should serve as warning signs to activists. They are warning signs that point not to the state of one's community but about the thinking of the individual activists themselves. They point to problems in not only particular organizing strategies but, more fundamentally, in the basic understanding particular activists of the overall process of organizing for social change.

Fighting for social change involves both organizing grassroots power to change the institutions of society and mobilizing one's own courage to change oneself. Activism must be both institution-transforming and self-transforming simultaneously. In the final section that follows, we examine why this is so important, especially in this critical period of world history.

Contemporary Activism

In this period of world history, activists in America face a special responsibility: that of not only engaging in our own self-transformation in the course of fighting for social change but also promoting the transformations in values and thinking of other Americans. The late Martin Luther King, Jr., best understood this special task. In the last two years of life, he called for a radical reconstruction of society and a radical revolution in values. He believed that activists in America could play a leading role in making this happen.

"The profit motive, when it is the sole basis of an economic system," he said, "encourages a cut-throat competition and selfish ambition that inspire men to be more I-centered than thou-centered. Equally, communism reduces men to a cog in the wheel of the state. . . . The good and just society is neither the thesis of capitalism nor the antithesis of communism, but a socially conscious democracy which reconciles the truths of individualism and collectivism."

"A true revolution of values," he continued, "will soon cause us to question the fairness and justice of many of our past and present policies" and to "see that an edifice which produces beggars needs restructuring. A true revolution of values will soon look uneasily on the glaring contrast of poverty and wealth. With righteous indignation, it will look overseas and see individual capitalists of the West investing huge sums of money in Asia, Africa and South America, only to take the profits out with no concern for the social betterment of the countries, and say, 'This is not just.' The Western arrogance of feeling that it has everything to teach others and nothing to learn from them is not just. A true revolution of values will . . . say of war, 'This way of settling differences is not just.'"

Thus, as we, as activists, participate in rallies and militantly oppose the oppressive old world order, we must not push into the background the importance of transforming our own values. In this post 9-11 period, especially, we must recognize the critical significance of spiritual values like compassion, generosity and community as "weapons" to combat militaristic world visions and corporate-driven material consumption.

8

Student Activism Has Waned in the United States

Doug Pennington

Doug Pennington is a staff reporter for The News Record *who writes on national issues.*

Activism among college students has declined dramatically in the United States. In fact, in the contemporary era, American students exercise very little political influence, especially when compared with their counterparts in other countries. Student organizations in the United States tend to work within established systems, rather than take to the street to protest. Large demonstrations are seen as counterproductive and likely to create more opposition to the goals of the activists. Nonetheless, mass mobilization continues to be an effective tool to influence elites and policymakers, as was demonstrated by large pro-immigration rallies in the United States in 2006.

The college student as a political force in the United States doesn't exist today.

If by the term "power" we mean the skill to make a decision with the leverage to enforce it, then the American college student has none.

Local Activist Efforts in Cincinnati

True, there are local exceptions where committed student leaders create something of value almost from scratch. The new University of Cincinnati Bearcat Transportation System is an example. Built on insider connections, cooperation rather than confrontation between powerful people and the semblance of popular support from a campus-wide referendum, this is a model of how a few students behind the scenes can get things done for a student population that largely doesn't care.

It would be fun, though, to watch a negotiation between administrators or state politicians and an elected student leader who could point out the window to 10,000 or 100,000 college students camped outside for the 10th day in a row.

That's the synergy of insider knowledge and a demonstrable popular strength that could get results on the most intractable problems—tuition, parking, even textbook prices.

In today's climate, it's almost impossible to imagine, even though nobody in power pays attention to people who have no leverage. I've tried to make this point in previous columns, especially in terms of collective fundraising strategies, but money is only a part of a comprehensive answer.

Mass Protests in France in 2006

Whatever you think of the merits of the student demonstrations going on now in France [in 2006] (I think they're trying to hold back a globalization wave with both hands), there is no denying their affect on the political process.

One- to three-million people on the streets apply a leverage that is different from, but no less potent than, a bundle of $2,000 checks handed to a politician's campaign committee. The freedoms of assembly and petition attract the very behaviors that threaten a government that respects those freedoms in the first place: violence and chaos.

The law-and-order types will naturally rise in defense of "reasonable debate" and public safety, and call such tactics "extortion." Except more often than not that's just code for "sit down, shut up and accept the status quo," coming from powerful people who want to stay in power, who also probably command a police force.

People have to be outraged by their circumstances enough to withstand the inevitable government response.

It is less the collection of vast numbers of people—in a "Kumbaya"-esque homage to liberty—that concentrates the minds of powerful individuals. Rather, it is the idea that they could lose control of a potentially volatile situation, the outcome of which few can predict, that invites attention to the multitudes and at least the appearance of compromise with them.

The Utility of Mass Demonstrations

We saw a version of that in the 1963 march on Washington. We saw it again [in 2006] in Los Angeles when some 500,000 people marched for fair immigration legislation.

We've also seen versions of it recently in France, Ukraine and Georgia—though not so much in Belarus. That country's president, Aleksandr Lukashenko, doesn't really care whether he looks like a gangster. While so far he's avoided a Tiananmen-style massacre in Minsk, Lukashenko has maintained his grip on power and jailed hundreds of people who protested his sham election last month.

The lesson: People have to be outraged by their circumstances enough to withstand the inevitable government response.

A half-million Hispanics and others demonstrate in Los Angeles for decent immigration policy. Over a million university students in France demonstrate for job security. College students here demonstrate for what?

With no contributions to political campaigns and no coordinated, massive public protest, students don't fight with two hands tied behind their backs. They don't fight at all.

9

Activism Has Been Crucial for the Environmental Movement

Mark Hertsgaard

Mark Hertsgaard is the environmental correspondent for The Nation *and a fellow at* The Nation Institute. *He is the author of* Earth Odyssey: Around the World in Search of Our Environmental Future *and* The Eagle's Shadow: Why America Fascinates and Infuriates the World.

Activism has dramatically changed the environmental movement by making it more diverse and broadening its appeal to the American people. Environmental activists have also become more politically aware and better able to form coalitions with other interest groups and influence policy debates. The 2004 election was a turning point that forced many traditional environmental activist groups to reassess their strategies and become more proactive. One element of the new approach has been a renewed emphasis on grassroots organizing and education. The result was a series of victories at the state level that reflected the growing political clout of the movement.

The most interesting environmental leader in the United States right now is a former petrochemical worker from Louisiana's "Cancer Alley" named Jerome Ringo. As chairman of the board of the National Wildlife Federation, Ringo heads what is by far the nation's largest environmental organization, with 4 million members, not to mention one of its richest, with an $80 million budget. It's unusual enough that a former

Mark Hertsgaard, "Green Goes Grassroots," *The Nation*, July 31, 2006, pp. 11–18. Reproduced by permission of the author.

union and community organizer would rise to the top of the NWF; traditionally, the group has belonged to the polite, apolitical wing of the movement more inclined to publish nature magazines for kids than to challenge corporate power à la Greenpeace or Rainforest Action Network. But what really sets Ringo apart, both at NWF and throughout the mainstream movement's leadership, is that he is black.

Diversifying Environmental Activism

"I am the first African-American in history to head a major conservation group," he says. Environmentalism in the United States has been dominated by well-to-do white men since the late nineteenth century, when John Muir, Gifford Pinchot and Teddy Roosevelt first put the notion of preserving natural resources on the national agenda with their campaigns to establish publicly owned parks and wilderness areas. Alluding to this history, Ringo says the whiteness of today's movement isn't because of racism. It's simply that most environmental groups "were founded by people who fished to put fish on the wall, not by people who fished to put fish on the table. And for poor people, issues like ozone depletion have not been a priority, compared with next month's rent. But I tell people in Cancer Alley, What good is next month's rent if you're dying from cancer?"

Now Ringo wants to bring these varying constituencies together across class and racial lines to build a broader and more powerful green movement. His chosen vehicle, besides the NWF, is the Apollo Alliance, a coalition of labor unions, environmental groups, business leaders and elected officials that advocates a massive green jobs and development program for the United States. Apollo proposes investing $300 billion of public funds in green energy technologies over the next ten years. This investment would create 3 million new jobs and countless business opportunities, Apollo claims, while also fighting climate change and cutting US dependence on foreign oil. The benefits to poor and working-class Americans of such an economic stimulus program are clear, but the idea is also business-friendly enough to have attracted support from prominent Democratic moderates and other centrists, including the group Republicans for Environmental Protection. "I had a phone call with the chief of staff of [New Mexico] Governor Bill Richardson just this morning," says Ringo, who assumed Apollo's presidency last September. "Several months ago I joined Hillary Clinton and [Pennsylvania] Governor Ed Rendell when the Democrats released their Energy Independence 2020 Plan, and one of the first items was an Apollo project. Apollo began five years ago as a vision. My goal is to turn it into action."

It's still too early to say, but if Jerome Ringo and the Apollo Alliance are representative of larger trends, green politics may at last be finding its voice again in the United States. In the past, most environmentalists did not bother to articulate much of an economic message. Perhaps because they tended to be economically comfortable themselves, they overlooked the fact that many Americans live paycheck to paycheck and thus need to hear that green policies can mean not only cleaner air but also more and better jobs. Indeed, environmentalists often failed to reach out to other constituencies at all; they stayed inside their own issue silo and assumed that having facts on their side was enough.

Increased Political Activism

"Our movement has been apolitical," says Brent Blackwelder, president of Friends of the Earth. "The idea was that politics is dirty and you don't want to get your hands dirty." Except for the Sierra Club and the League of Conservation Voters, environmentalists shunned electoral politics in particular. Green groups did not even turn out their own members to vote, much less boost turnout among ordinary citizens. When the outrages of the Bush Administration finally led some groups to consider taking a more active role in the 2004 elections, internal polling found that the 10 million members of national environmental groups voted at the same low turnout rates as the general population. "Some groups' members didn't even know there was much difference between Bush and Kerry on the environment," adds Blackwelder.

"No one feels the pain when they vote against the environment. They should," says Wendy Wendlandt, political director of the National Association of State Public Interest Research Groups. Noting that no politician, including Bush, wants to be seen as anti-environment, Wendlandt adds that the movement must "regain control over what it means to be environmentalist. We need to pick bright-line issues that define who is for you and who is against you and then hold elected officials accountable."

The 2004 Election

Bush's November 2004 victory jolted environmentalists, as did the nearly simultaneous release of Michael Shellenberger and Ted Nordhaus's essay "The Death of Environmentalism." First reported in *The Nation*, the essay argued that the movement was failing because it remained wedded to timid, technical-fix solutions that ignored potential allies and left ordinary people uninspired and confused. In the ensuing storm of argument, many greens responded that they had been saying as much for years. Others pointed out that Shellenberger and Nordhaus defined the movement very narrowly, ignoring thousands of state and local, environmental justice, anti-corporate and other grassroots organizations. The essay "reads more accurately and less offensively" if one realizes that when "the authors use the words 'environmental movement' they are actually talking about large budget" national organizations based in Washington, DC, wrote John Sellers of the Ruckus Society and Steve Kretzmann of Oil Change. Those groups were indeed "locked into a costly and near futile legislatively dominated strategy," they added, but small and medium-sized groups were still driving change through local organizing and protest. To support their case that change in Washington tends to come "only after a lot of noise has been made, and attitudes have changed in the field," Sellers and Kretzmann cited a study by Jon Agnone of the University of Washington, who analyzed Congressional passage of environmental laws in the United States from 1960 to 1998. Agnone concluded that shifts in public opinion did help get legislation passed, but only when accompanied by visible acts of grassroots protest.

[T]here has been an explosion of student activism, particularly around global warming. . .

What no one disputes is that the movement's glory days of the 1960s and '70s seem long ago and far away. Back then, mass awareness and targeted activism propelled Washington politicians of both parties to enact a series of landmark laws including the National Environmental Policy Act, the Clean Air Act and the Clean Water Act that transformed America's ecosystems and were copied by nations around the world. Ronald Reagan began the environmental rollback in the 1980s, and the Clinton Administration regained little ground in the '90s. But it is George W. Bush's Administration, with its overt hostility to environmentalism, that best highlights an embarrassing paradox for the movement. Opinion polls indicate that more than 70 percent of American people think we as a society should do "whatever it takes" to protect the environment. And no one can say the environmental movement lacks financial resources; the budgets of local and national groups amount to an estimated $1.7 billion a year. Nevertheless, Bush and his congressional allies have pursued the most anti-environmental policies in the nation's history—and escaped without paying much of a political price. As popular and wealthy as the environmental movement appears, the Bush era has exposed it as something of a paper tiger.

Yet the Bush years may turn out to be the movement's salvation, for they have led even the national groups based in Washington to recognize that a new approach is needed. And political space has now opened around climate change in particular. Hurricane Katrina, combined with a relentless accumulation of scientific findings, has at last awakened both the public and elites in the United States to the gravity of the threat. How else to explain how Al Gore, a man the media mercilessly mocked as dull, pretentious and untrustworthy during his 2000 presidential campaign, is now being treated as one of the hottest politicians in America, thanks largely to his starring role in the climate change documentary *An Inconvenient Truth*.

State and Local Movements

There are successes to learn from. The federal government is a dead end at the moment, but state and local environmental organizations are scoring solid victories in red and blue states alike. Meanwhile, years of pressure have led a surprising number of big-name corporations, including such longstanding villains as General Electric and Wal-Mart, to make and sometimes honor promises to change their operating practices thanks to a good cop, bad cop routine that offers them a choice between the in-your-face denunciations issued by groups like Global Exchange and Forest Ethics and the genteel green tutelage offered by the World Resources Institute and World Wildlife Fund. Environmental justice groups like West Harlem Environmental Action are developing real political clout while proving that affluent white people aren't the only ones who care about clean air and water. And there has been an explosion of student activism, particularly around global warming, which Billy Parish, coordinator of the Climate Action Coalition, calls "far and away the biggest issue on campuses now, and not only for environmental groups. There are now 200 campuses purchasing substantial amounts of clean energy."

The huge successes of the 1970s were built on decades of work, a lot of it done at the local level, around issues and concerns that then were taken national.

The successes have a number of themes in common, beginning with a focus on economically attractive solutions rather than downbeat warnings of disaster. "As scary as things look nowadays, we have decided to spend half of our time building the new—showing how to solve these problems and have a better life in the bargain—rather than always playing defense," says Betsy Taylor, founder of the Center for a New American Dream. Another key has been reaching out to new and sometimes ideologically or culturally distant constituencies, and doing so in plain language that ordinary people can grasp (rather than the policy-wonk gibberish that environmentalists often utter). A third element has been an emphasis on sustained local organizing that grows the movement's base of support and seeks to build real political power—a departure from many groups' reliance on activist insiders skilled in lobbying, litigation and other tactics aimed at the status quo.

The 1960s and 1970s

One hesitates to dust off the cliché, but together the strategies recall the 1960s slogan "Think globally, act locally." The stress on organizing begins to correct a mistake that progressive movements made in the wake of the high-profile victories of the 1960s, argues Van Jones, executive director of the Ella Baker Center for Human Rights. As grants from mainstream foundations began boosting budgets dramatically, says Jones, the civil rights movement became a civil rights bureaucracy, staffed with lobbyists and lawyers who increasingly tried to stand in for a demobilized black community. The same happened with other progressive movements, with the result, Jones adds, that over time "most of us spent more time writing grant applications and doing work that had nothing to do with building political power."

"The huge successes of the 1970s were built on decades of work, a lot of it done at the local level, around issues and concerns that then were taken national. We've been drawing down on these capital reserves ever since then without rebuilding them at the local level," says Buck Parker, executive director of Earthjustice and current chair of the Green Group, made up of leaders from thirty national environmental groups who convene regularly to discuss strategy and tactics.

It was self-deceptive for environmentalists to think they enjoyed support from 70 percent of the American public, argues Carl Pope, executive director of the Sierra Club. A keener analysis of polling data, says Pope, reveals that about 40 percent of the public are pro-environment but not pro-environmentalist. These 40 percent take green positions on policy questions (e.g., Do you support action on global warming?), but culturally "they see us as too extreme. They tend to be more rural and conservative but also include significant numbers of urban, nonwhite and less educated people. The right effectively split them off from us in the 1980s and '90s, and we did nothing to prevent this. We didn't build good relationships with churches, labor unions and African-American and Latino constituencies." Concludes Pope, "Our challenge is to reknit the environmental majority, because it's still there, it's just been artificially divided." The place to start is at the state level, where activists are passing "amazing legislation that we couldn't even talk about with the Democratic caucus on Capitol Hill. Idaho just enacted a two-year ban on coal-fired power plants. The Idaho governor, who is now Bush's new Interior Secretary, didn't want to do it, but the legislature rolled him. Maryland, with a Republican governor, has signed on to the Kyoto Protocol."

Colorado 2004

"In 2004 Kerry lost Colorado, but we won everything else here," says Elise Jones, executive director of the Colorado Environmental Coalition. Jones's group was a key member of a broader progressive coalition that, in a state with a majority of Republican voters, passed three progressive ballot initiatives, took back the state legislature and won the US Senate seat. "Seeing how the conservatives who orchestrated the Gingrich revolution [in 1994] went back to the grassroots made me realize that we needed to do the same thing," says Jones.

Leaders of the national groups say they are returning to the grassroots, mainly by collaborating more with state and local organizations.

The key in Colorado was to "appeal to people across the political spectrum" by addressing their concerns as much as environmentalists' own. To pass the renewable energy initiative, progressives won over economically strapped farmers in the east of Colorado, who have traditionally voted Republican, by stressing how wind farms could help them pay their bills. Even the Farm Bureau, usually environmentalists' enemy, ended up backing the initiative, as did the Republican Speaker of the House.

Michigan and Florida

A similar green upsurge has taken place in Michigan. "For fifteen years we counted it as a success if we could just protect the status quo," says Lana Pollack, president of the Michigan Environmental Council. "Now we actually move the ball down the field. And we have a Republican House and Senate and a Democratic governor, so we have to move things through both parties." Much of the change comes from implementing what Pollack concedes are Politics 101 tactics. "You have to work at the ground level. We turn out thousands of letters to get constituents informed and revved up. We don't put out dense reports but shorter, more newsworthy releases. We stopped looking at everyone outside the environmental world as the hostile, unwashed masses and saw them as distinct interests that on occasion might align with ours, including nurses groups, business groups and the Michigan Association of Realtors."

Leaders of national groups say they too are returning to the grassroots, mainly by collaborating more with state and local organizations. "It was critical to be in Washington the last few years to resist the [Bush] rollback, which we've done," says Frances Beinecke, president of the Natural Resources Defense Council. But when the Administration proposed allowing inadequately treated sewage to drain into coastal runoff systems, Beinecke adds, NRDC "took the issue out of Washington to a state that would be severely affected by that proposal, Florida, and worked it there. We put local groups like the Florida Federation of Garden Clubs out front to raise awareness of the issue, and we got eighteen out of twenty-five members of the Florida Congressional delegation to come out against it, including very conservative members like Katherine Harris."

10

Activists Can Go Too Far Using Violence and Illegal Means to Achieve Their Aims

John J. Miller

John J. Miller is a political journalist for the National Review *and a contributing editor for the magazine* Reason. *He is the author of* The Unmaking of Americans: How Multiculturalism Has Undermined America's Assimilation Ethic.

Some activists have incorporated violence or attacks on property in their campaigns to change policy. Certain animal rights groups have utilized "direct action" in order to stop testing and experiments on non-human species such as dogs, primates, and mice or other rodents. Such violent acts are forms of terrorism that cannot be ignored even though the activists may have laudable goals. Instead, the activists cause widespread damage and destroy valuable research, while harming individual researchers who are simply doing their jobs. The result is that the very goals of the activists are undermined while their tactics are opposed by the public.

Six days after the World Trade Center was destroyed, the New York Stock Exchange rang its opening bell and traders sang "God Bless America" from the floor: They wanted to send a loud-and-clear message to the world that al-Qaeda could not shut down the U.S. economy. Even though the Dow suffered its biggest one-day point-loss in history, the mere fact

John J. Miller, "In the Name of the Animals," *National Review*, vol. 59, July 2006, pp. 38–40. Copyright © 2006 by *National Review*, Inc., 215 Lexington Avenue, New York, NY 10016. Reproduced by permission.

that buying and selling could resume so quickly marked an inspiring day for capitalism and against terrorism.

Activism and Terrorism

On September 7, 2005, however, terrorists struck again, and the NYSE still hasn't recovered. This time, they didn't target a couple of skyscrapers near the exchange, but rather a company called Life Sciences Research (LSR). It had recently qualified for a NYSE listing and its senior management had gathered on Wall Street to celebrate the occasion. Just a few minutes before the first trades were set to occur, NYSE president Catherine Kinney informed her guests that their listing would be postponed. It was immediately obvious to everyone from LSR what had happened: "A handful of animal extremists had succeeded where Osama bin Laden had failed," Mark Bibi, the company's general counsel, would say in congressional testimony the next month.

[T]he FBI said that 35 of its offices were conducting more than 150 investigations into 'animal rights/eco-terrorist activities'.

LSR is better known by the name of its operating subsidiary, Huntingdon Life Sciences (HLS), which is in the business of testing products on animals to assess their safety and comply with government regulations. Most people probably don't like to think about what goes on in these labs—vivisections of monkeys, for instance—but they also appreciate the importance of research whose ultimate goal is the protection and enhancement of human health. About 95 percent of all lab animals are rats and mice, but for animal-rights extremists who believe that "a rat is a pig is a dog is a boy" (as Ingrid Newkirk of People for the Ethical Treatment of Animals once said), the whole endeavor is deeply immoral. And some of them have decided that because the traditional practices of honest persuasion and civil disobedience haven't changed many hearts or minds, they must now adopt a different strategy—something they euphemistically call "direct action." These are efforts to intimidate and harass animal researchers and everyone who comes into contact with them. In recent years, hardcore activists have embraced property destruction and physical assaults. "This is the number-one domestic terrorist threat in America," says Sen. James Inhofe, an Oklahoma Republican. Keeping LSR off the Big Board probably represents their greatest achievement yet.

Bad Tactics

The animal-rights movement may be wrongheaded, but there's no denying that most of its members are motivated by genuine compassion for animals and a sincere commitment to preventing cruelty. There's also no denying that violence in their name has become a significant problem. Just as the pro-life movement is haunted by the murderers of abortion doctors, the environmental and animal-rights movements are cursed by their own packs of fierce radicals. A year ago, the FBI said that 35 of its offices were conducting more than 150 investigations into "animal rights/eco-terrorist activities." The number of illegal incidents involving these activities has risen sharply, from 220 in the 1980s and 1990s to 363 in just the last five years, according to a recent report by the Foundation for Biomedical Research, an association of businesses and universities that conduct animal research. (By contrast, abortion-clinic violence appears to be subsiding.)

"Other groups don't come close in terms of the financial damage they've done," says John Lewis, an FBI agent who until recently coordinated federal efforts against domestic terrorism. Not even militants in the mold of Timothy McVeigh, the man behind the Oklahoma City bombing in 1995? "We have an acute interest in all of these groups, but when the rubber meets the road, the eco- and animal-rights terrorists lately have been way out in front." Lewis estimates that they've caused around $100 million in damage, mostly property destruction affecting businesses, much of it from arson. This fall, eleven defendants will face trial in Oregon for causing an estimated $20 million in damage in five states.

Animal Rights Attacks

Although animal-rights terrorism is fundamentally barbaric, its execution has assumed increasingly sophisticated forms. The campaign against Huntingdon Life Sciences began in the United Kingdom seven years ago with the formation of a group called Stop Huntingdon Animal Cruelty, or SHAC. Soon after, SHAC recruited members in the United States to focus on an HLS facility in New Jersey, using methods that were deployed to great effect in the U.K. A federal trial earlier this year—perhaps the most important trial ever held involving animal-rights extremism—put the group's methods on full display.

Many of SHAC's efforts targeted HLS directly. An electronic attack in 2002, for instance, caused the HLS server to overload. But other confrontations involved HLS employees away from work: cars vandalized in driveways, rocks tossed through the windows of homes, and graffiti messages such as "PUPPY KILLER" spray-painted on houses. Descriptions of these incidents were dutifully posted on SHAC's own website, often with an unnerving sense of glee. After a tire-slashing visit to the home of one HLS employee, for example, the SHACtivists seemed pleased that "his wife is reportedly on the brink of a nervous breakdown and divorce." These messages were meant to generate publicity, build a sense of momentum, and serve as models for activists spread across the country. In Britain, one top HLS employee was attacked by a group of hooded men wielding ax handles. "It's only a matter of time before it happens in the United States," warns Frankie Trull, head of the Foundation for Biomedical Research. "Everything they do over there eventually comes over here."

Sometimes protestors would gather in front of her [Marion Helos's] house, banging drums and hollering into megaphones.

Intimidating employees in their private lives places pressure on HLS itself. But SHAC's harassment didn't stop with HLS employees. They also engaged in "tertiary targeting"— i.e., taking aim at companies with ties to HLS, plus their workers. Dozens of firms decided that doing business with HLS simply wasn't worth it. Deloitte & Touche, which had audited the HLS books, ended its relationship. Lawn gardeners quit. Even a security company that provided services to HLS succumbed to the abuse.

Intimidation

SHAC's methods certainly can be menacing, as transcripts from the trial make clear. One of SHAC's main targets was Marsh, a company that sold insurance to HLS. There was a smoke-bomb attack at an office in Seattle, forcing the evacuation of a high-rise building. In San Antonio, SHAC members glued the locks to a Marsh office and plastered the windows and doors of the building with pictures of a mutilated dog. Once they even stormed inside, screaming threats: "You have the blood of death on your hands!

We know where you live! You cannot sleep at night! We will find you!"

And they made good on these threats. Marsh employees were repeatedly harassed at home. There were late-night phone calls: "Are you scared? Do you think the puppies should be scared?" Other calls were more menacing: "We know where you live. You shouldn't sleep at night. You shouldn't rest until the puppies rest." Marion Harlos, who was managing director for Marsh in San Antonio, said that people went through her mail, ordered magazine subscriptions in her name, and rang her doorbell and dashed off in a kind of never-ending Devil's Night. Sometimes protesters would gather in front of her house, banging drums and hollering into megaphones. "They proceeded to parade the neighborhood, shout my name, that of my children," she said. "I was petrified. I was petrified for my children." The kids were kept indoors: "We did not know what was going to take place. Would someone be in the front yard? Would someone be in the back yard? Would someone come up and talk to them? Would someone try and take them?" To make a bad situation even worse, a neighbor threatened to sue Harlos, claiming that the ongoing presence of protesters was hurting property values. Harlos eventually moved.

Sally Dillenback, a Marsh employee in Dallas, had a similarly harrowing experience. A SHAC website published private information, some of it probably obtained by going through her trash: her home address, her car's license-plate number, and even her auto-insurance policy number. Most unsettling, however, was the information about her children: their names, the names of their schools and teachers, and descriptions of their after-school activities. "I felt that my family might be threatened with that kind of information being posted," she testified. The activists certainly didn't leave her alone; they plastered pictures on the side of her house, her mailbox, and her sidewalk. A SHAC website described the strategy: "Let the stickers serve to remind Marsh employees and their neighbors that their homes are paid for in the blood, the blood of innocent animals." On other occasions, animal-rights radicals held protests outside her home with drums and bullhorns. They followed her to church. The scariest moment may have been when Dillenback read an e-mail: "It asked how I would feel if they cut open my son . . . and filled him with poison the way that they, Huntingdon, [were] doing to animals." Her husband bought a semi-automatic shotgun, even though Mrs. Dillenback doesn't like guns: "He was wanting to protect the family."

Victims

Marsh employees were by no means the only tertiary victims of abuse. Two bombs went off at a California office of Chiron, a biotech company. Nobody was hurt, but the second explosion was delayed—a tactic sometimes used by terrorists to kill first responders. Workers at GlaxoSmithKline, a pharmaceutical company, also had their windows smashed and mail stolen. In one case, SHAC posted information about the spouse of a GSK employee who was undergoing treatment for alcoholism. Another employee was summoned to the Baltimore morgue to identify a dead relative—but when she arrived, she learned the call was a hoax.

Sometimes, the connections between SHAC targets and HLS were so tenuous as to be almost nonexistent. Elaine Perna, a housewife who is married to an executive who retired from the Bank of New York—another company with ties to HLS—confronted SHAC when protesters appeared on her porch. "When I opened the door, they were yelling at me through the bullhorn. One spat at my face through the screen and yelled obscenities at me, about me, about my husband." A defense lawyer's attempt to minimize the incident—"All Ms. Gazzola did was she screamed through the bullhorn, didn't she?"—irritated Perna: "They were yelling at me through a bullhorn, they were calling me effing this and my husband effing that and spitting in my face through a screen. Now, if you think that 'that's all,' you know, you can call it 'that's all.' But to me, it wasn't 'that's all.'" The mayhem didn't stop until the police arrived.

On March 2, a jury convicted six members of SHAC (at press time, sentencing had not yet occurred). This is an important victory, but animal-rights extremism isn't going away—groups such as Hugs for Puppies and Win Animal

Rights are now on the scene, continuing their perverse crusade. They certainly don't lack for true believers. In Senate testimony last fall, Jerry Vlasak of the North American Animal Liberation Press Office announced that violence against HLS was "extensional self-defense" in behalf of "non-human animals." Recently, a mysterious full-page advertisement appeared in the *New York Times* and the *Wall Street Journal*. It featured the image of a man in a black ski mask, alongside the words "I Control Wall Street" and a short account of the NYSE fiasco. "Nobody knows who paid for it," says Trull. One theory proposes that a group of institutional investors are responsible, another claims that it's a backhanded attempt by animal-rights activists to raise anxieties even further. HLS still isn't listed.

Several members of Congress have tried to address this species of domestic terrorism by proposing legislation that would toughen the Animal Enterprise Protection Act, a law that was passed before the advent of "tertiary targeting." At the recent trial, prosecutors secured convictions against SHAC only because they were able to rely on anti-stalking laws. "They had to scour the federal code, looking for violations," says Brent McIntosh, a deputy assistant attorney general at the Department of Justice. "This is an enormous, surreptitious, and interstate conspiracy. We need to strengthen laws against it." Bills to do so have been introduced in both the House and the Senate, but a crowded legislative calendar probably means they won't be debated until a new Congress convenes next year.

The stakes are high. "Five years from now, we don't want to count up another $100 million in losses," says the FBI's Lewis. That's true, although the real costs of animal-rights terrorism aren't really quantifiable. They come in the form of medical discoveries that are delayed or never made, products that aren't approved, and careers that aren't started. Whatever the real price tag, one thing is certain: Each time an animal-rights terrorist wins, people lose.

11

Activism Is Most Effective as a Grassroots Movement

Hilda Kurtz

Hilda Kurtz is an assistant professor of geography at the University of Georgia where her research focuses on environmental justice and gender issues.

Often poor and ethnic minority communities face an unequal share of environmental and industrial pollution. In St. James Parish, Louisiana, the citizens of the community banded together to prevent the construction of a chemical plant that would have polluted a local river. The success of the community activists was based on their knowledge of the area and familiarity with the people. They formed a variety of action groups and fought both the industrial company and state officials in an effort to save their parish.

In 1996, a company called Shintech, Inc. (an American subsidiary of Japanese Shin-Etsu Chemical Company) applied for the environmental permits necessary to build an integrated polyvinylchloride (PVC) production facility in the rural parish township of Convent. St. James Parish is located at the centre of Louisiana's Mississippi River industrial corridor, an 84-mile corridor of concentrated petrochemical production, home to 137 facilities reporting to [Enviromental Protection Agency] (EPA's) Toxic Release Inventory (TRI facilities). The Convent site offered the company excellent access to raw ma-

Hilda Kurtz, "Alternative Visions for Citizenship Practice in an Environmental Justice Dispute," *Space and Polity*, vol. 9, April 2005, pp. 77–78, 84–88. Reproduced by permission of Taylor & Francis, Ltd, www.informaworld.com.

terials, transport, markets for by-products and agglomeration economies; these attractions were compounded by offers of substantial tax incentives to build on the site. If built, the Shintech plant would contribute 2,000 temporary jobs and 165 technician and 90 maintenance jobs on a permanent basis. The PVC plant would also contribute over 600,000 pounds of air pollution (vinyl chloride, benzene, chlorine and ammonia, among others) to the emissions from 10 existing TRI facilities (8 petrochemical facilities, a sugar refinery and an iron processing plant).

Community Reaction to Shintech

Shintech's announcement was met with mixed reactions among parish residents. Some people welcomed the prospect of adding jobs to the local economy. Parish unemployment levels hovered between 10 and 14 percent through the early 1990s. Others reacted with concern about yet another source of toxic emissions in the already heavily burdened parish. The parish had ranked third highest in toxic air emissions in Louisiana's TRI for several years, while Louisiana consistently ranked either first or second on the national TRI (alternating ranks with Texas). Parish residents were predominantly low-income and 49 percent of them were African Americans (compared with 33 percent of the state population), few were likely to benefit directly from the 165 technically expert jobs the facility would create.

A local community group called the St. James Citizens for Jobs and the Environment formed in order to protest against the environmental permits for the facility, and networked with larger community, environmental, civil rights and environmental justice organisations to argue that the community did not need or want any more petrochemical facilities. The group's members invoked, in part, their identities as citizens to press a claim of environmental injustice against the facility. Significantly, the language of citizenship they brought to bear on the environmental justice (EJ) dispute drew simultaneously from multiple discourses of citizenship identity and practice. On the one hand, the St. James Citizens invoked liberal individual citizenship by arguing that siting the facility would violate their civil rights, and by calling for an equitable distribution of pollution within a largely distributive paradigm. On the other hand, the group's emphasis on local autonomy and self-determination went well beyond the procedural equity called for by legal scholars, invoking a recognisably communitarian tradition of citizenship. . . .

Citizen Activists

The six women who started the St. James Citizens could have called themselves Residents of Convent (their town) or Mothers of St. James, but they did not. Instead, they invoked the idea of citizenship in a democratic society to broaden the scope of their protest beyond that of a local siting conflict and argued that they should have a voice in the future economic development of their community. Using this rhetoric, they grew the organisation to a diverse membership of more than 100 people (young, old, Black, White, men, women, working, retired, etc.).

The flexible invocation of citizenship by which opponents of the proposed Shintech facility fought for inclusion in public debate over the facility is best understood by distinguishing between the formal and the sociocultural dimensions of citizenship. Formal provisions for citizen participation, structured as invitations for general public comment at particular intervals in the environmental permitting process, were inadequate to the group's vision of themselves as citizens embedded in a political community under threat. From the outset of the controversy, the St. James Citizens invoked a set of sociocultural understandings of citizenship that were embedded in the scale of the community. They used a community-oriented language of citizenship to privilege a high degree of local input and even self-determination with respect to economic development. Their community-based argument centred on rejecting the state's zero-sum approach that pitted jobs against environmental protection. The state government was fast-tracking the environmental permitting process for the facility, on the premise that it would bring much-needed jobs and value-added manufacturing capacity to the state. The local group and a growing coalition of other organisations called into question not only the suitability of the proposed facility, but the legitimacy of the state government's stance, and pointedly suggested in public statements and elsewhere that local communities could do the job of local economic development better than could the state. Arguing against the state of Louisiana's embrace of petrochemical development in the river parishes, for example, one of the St. James Citizens exclaimed

> Let's look at the parish . . . Let's look at the last 30 years of development. Has it accomplished what we as a community envisioned that it would? [No.] Do we want to continue in that same direction, or perhaps do we want to steer our community differently? . . . [We need to] get this whole community to participate in what is your vision for this community? How can we make this community the best possible community? Building on what we have naturally. . . . Who are we as a people, who are we as a community?

This language suggests not the citizenship of negative freedoms implicit in the liberal project, but a citizenship that values political process and citizen participation in steering the affairs of the political community. While the local community as an entity had never been given an opportunity to plan for its future in the way implied, the words conjure a compelling vision of local self-determination. . . .

Hurdles Faced By Activists

Significantly, the legal and administrative strategy available to the St. James Citizens through formal provisions for citizen participation did not fit the sociospatial construction of the problem embedded in this community-oriented critique. The state's environmental agency was not likely to recognise or legitimate the group's vision of community self-determination. Local citizens prepared public comments in the state-level environmental permitting process, but their comments were not privileged over those of anyone else. In fact, the company flew in dozens of staff members and consultants to weight the public record of comments in their favour.

Local citizens prepared public comments in the state-level environmental permitting process, but their comments were not privileged over those of anyone else.

In the face of such limitations, the St. James Citizens secured representation by the Tulane Environmental Law Clinic and filed an environmental justice complaint with the U.S. Environmental Protection Agency. In a sharp shift from their community-centred starting-point, their federal environmental justice claim focused on distributive equity ensconced in a liberal conception of rights. The St. James Citizens and a coalition of other groups argued that the state's environmental permitting practices produced a disparate impact of pollution on people of colour, violating EPA's regulations under Title VI of the Civil Rights Act of 1964. Title VI mandates that recipients of federal funds—in this case, the state environmental agency—must not conduct programmes or activities in ways which produce racially disparate impacts. The St. James Citizens' Title VI complaint argued that the Louisiana Department of Environmental Quality's approval of Shintech and six existing facilities within a four-mile radius of the Shintech site, in a predominantly African American area, constituted a racially disparate burden of pollution and was a clear case of environmental racism. The population living within 4 miles of the Shintech site was 81 per cent African American. The EPA took on the Shintech protesters' claim as a test case for agency's emerging environmental justice framework. The Shintech protesters maintained dual discourses of citizenship from that point onwards; the distributive claim of the Title VI complaint moved the legal process forward, while the procedural claim took shape largely outside the legal context, in public representations of the group's agenda in informal arenas such as public protests. Under these conditions, subject-citizens, communities and the public-private divide were constructed in tension between liberal and communitarian interpretive frameworks for the remainder of the controversy.

The population living within 4 miles of the Shintech site was 81 percent African American.

The EPA and Environmental Racism

The potential siting of the Shintech facility was now formally a distributive problem before the EPA, for the agency to use as a test case for developing a spatial (distributive) approach. When responding to a Title VI complaint of environmental racism, EPA analysts must evaluate whether the state-sanctioned distribution of environmental hazards constitutes a disparate impact on people of colour. Analysts aggregate, divide and buffer geographical space to reach an assessment of the equitability of the burden of pollution in a given locale. EPA defines the spatial boundaries of polluted districts with higher than the national average of people of colour and people of low income, and evaluates the social suitability of a proposed facility for a given site, based on considerations of equity. These spatial boundaries in turn have implications for whether and how people living nearby have access to decision-making processes. If persons live within the enumeration boundaries of an area that meets certain criteria, then they have better access to formal standing in an environmental justice complaint than those who live outside such boundaries. . . .

Significantly, however, while the quest for equal access to non-toxic environments stems from interpreting the promise of egalitarianism as spatial equity, calls for environmental justice move beyond the premises of liberalism to demand a safe place not for individuals as such, but for communities—defined both socially and geographically. In this case, equal access to a certain kind of space (for example, non-polluted space) is not conceptualised as an individual right, but as a right that should be accorded a geographically defined group of people. On this point, the collective social space constructed in a communitarian rhetoric of environmental justice diverges from the individualised social space that is constructed in a rhetoric of individual liberalism and evaluated in state-sanctioned spatial analyses.

Liberal and communitarian interpretive frameworks traced in this dispute also produced a tension concerning the line(s) between public and private realms of social life. While the liberal perspective delineates quite starkly between the two, the line is rather blurred in the 'embodiment' of the communitarian citizen in the political community. The Shintech protesters themselves challenged the line drawn by liberal citizenship between public and private space/spheres. The St. James Citizens grew as a protest group when neighbours realised that their family health problems were being experienced in households across the parish. Experience of private health problems coalesced into the political representation of respiratory and cancer-related illnesses in their parish as a public health problem. They attributed the frequency of ill health to the presence of 10 TRI facilities in their parish and many more TRI facilities upwind in adjacent Ascension Parish. The St. James Citizens' attempts to place their household and community concerns squarely in the sphere of public debate, met with attempts on the part of state officials to remove their concerns to the margins of that debate, where they could disappear into the private sphere. State officials did so in more than one forum by dismissing the leaders of the St. James Citizens for Jobs and Environment, for instance, as "just a bunch of housewives" and their leader as "a very simple woman".

Strategies and Tactics

The St. James Citizens for Jobs and Environment refused to be marginalised on gendered or any other terms and continued to press the point that what could be considered private health problems raised important issues about public health, economic development and citizens' rights. For example, the St. James Citizens took issue with the parish and state policy called Shelter in Place in which area residents are instructed over the radio and public announcement systems to close up their homes and stay inside when an accidental or excessive release of toxic air emissions occurs. Shelter in Place guidelines call for residents to remain in their homes while air toxins dissipate; this can take the better part of a day. Many residents resented both the absurdity of seeking shelter in older, modest and poorly insulated homes, and the isolation they felt from the rest of the community while confined indoors. Playing on the notion of home as a locus for their concerns, they challenged the liberal divide between the public and private realms by inviting state environmental officials to stay with them in their homes for a week, so that these officials might better understand the daily experience of exposure to airborne toxic emissions, including days of elevated emissions in which the air is acrid and tinted blue or green. State policymakers had long minimised the importance of any environmental and health impacts of the petrochemical industry by invoking the need for the industry's relatively high-paying jobs in the state economy. In the local activists' view, decision-makers could afford to do so, because they were physically removed from the reality of a cumulative burden of industrial pollution. Inviting decision-makers to stay with members of the group for a week was intended to erase the effect of that distance and to show them how everyday mobility was affected by perceptions of risk.

State officials declined the invitation. While this was a reasonable response from the perspective of public employees who expect some insulation from 'the field' that they oversee, it was a further sign to the St. James Citizens that their own perspective of the problem at hand was far different from that of the bureaucrats in the Louisiana Department of Environmental Quality (LDEQ). The St. James Citizens' perspective on the need for environmental justice in St. James Parish had blurred public and private lives and spaces in collective defence of the 'community'.

While making use of provisions for EPA to review the distributive effects of LDEQ's permitting practices, the St. James Citizens continued to press for a more deeply community-based form of procedural justice, in which bureaucrats cared as much as they did about their community and empowered them to exercise local autonomy in fostering a safer, healthier future. The EPA was caught in the middle of a very heated political debate and was seen by many to be stalling for time, as it delayed decision after decision in the case. In a partial victory for the environmental justice activists involved, Shintech withdrew its environmental permit applications for the site in September 1998 and moved ahead with plans to build a smaller facility in another parish 40 miles upriver.

12

Activism Is Best When Grassroot Organizations Work with Local Officials

John Baranski

John Baranski is an assistant professor of history at Fort Lewis College in Durango, Colorado, where he researches public housing issues.

During the 1960s, an activist movement for better housing emerged among the residents of San Francisco's public housing community. Resident activists sought to not only improve their quality of life, but to also have a greater say in decisions and planning for their neighborhoods. The activists initially met with resistance from government officials, but were later able to forge a partnership with local politicians which allowed for the community to achieve its goals. The example highlights the importance of activists and local officials working together to better communities.

During the 1960s and 1970s, in response to crumbling housing, a shortage of jobs and affordable homes, and general neglect from city officials and employers, tenant activism in San Francisco's public housing increased dramatically. Women, more than men, led this movement at the building, city, and national level. Tenants demanded more and better public housing, useful jobs, and an expansion of child, elderly,

John Baranski, "Something to Help Themselves: Tenant Organizing in San Francisco's Public Housing, 1965–1975," *Journal of Urban History*, vol. 33, March 2007, pp. 418–421, 433–436. Republished with permission of Sage Publications, Inc., conveyed through Copyright Clearance Center, Inc.

and health care. They even demanded control of San Francisco Housing Authority (SFHA) funds and hiring. Tenant organizing occurred within and contributed to a rich urban context of community action programs, civil rights struggles, and movements against authority at home and abroad. SFHA officials did not always share the same vision as tenants, but they nevertheless provided housing authority resources and support to tenant organizing. Tenants constructed a political identity around their place and status as they organized around a vision of economic and civil rights that was at odds with the views of some city leaders and a growing number of federal policy makers.

Tenant Activism

That vision had much in common with tenants in other North American cities. . . . In the United States, tenants had to contend with a mixed housing market and legal system that favored property owners over renters. The Department of Housing and Urban Development (HUD) and Lyndon B. Johnson's Great Society programs offered more promises than programs, more constraints than possibilities to address structural inequality in housing, social services, and employment. As with other social movements of the era, the experiences of tenants and their allies in San Francisco produced both hope and frustration. The ideas and actions of San Francisco's public housing tenants revealed a willingness to turn democratic values into action. Breaking popular and academic stereotypes of an underclass mired in a culture of poverty, their activities in housing and urban development helped to produce a vision of community in which citizens and residents had meaningful employment, vital social and human services, and economic security. In these ways, San Francisco's tenants were out of step with the trajectory of the nation's social policy and liberal political culture.

Since World War II, SFHA tenants had tried to influence public housing policies individually and collectively. But SFHA executive secretary director John Beard had discouraged, Red-baited, and even punished tenant organizers. His reluctance to listen to collective demands of tenants, embrace civil rights, and expand and improve the authority's housing stock won him few admirers. Beard's power waned in the early 1960s as tenants formed unions and associations. By 1965, tenant representatives were appearing before the five-member SFHA commission, demanding better building maintenance, a more responsive authority staff, and improvements such as better swing sets and lighting. They also organized recreational and cultural activities and made policy recommendations to the SFHA and other city agencies. Alma Burleigh, secretary of the North Beach Improvement Association, said her association has improved our "living conditions. . . . We have an exciting program of activities for children and adults. We have initiated new and more friendly relations between all tenants, between tenants and management and the Commission. The tenants in this project have begun to develop a new spirit of enthusiasm and optimism concerning their homes." She continued, "people in public housing have begun to do something to help themselves."

Early Success

Tenants also set their sights on John Beard. Following a blistering Fair Employment Practices Commission (FEPC) report on the authority's failure to fairly administer housing and employment and amid dramatic collective actions around the world for human rights and self-determination, SFHA tenants formulated a plan to oust Beard. On October 7, 1965, they assembled community allies at a packed SFHA commission meeting at which tenant union representatives Audrey Smith, Mary Louise Paddock, Constance Lotti, and a Mrs. Washington presented a list of grievances. Paddock, who represented three thousand public housing tenants through the Sunnydale Citizens' League, took the microphone to demand immediate action on repair orders, more effective pest controls, new paint and clotheslines, and adequate lighting for safety. She also expected the authority to deliver more child care. Smith, Washington, and Lotti articulated similar concerns and expectations. Their collective testimony prepared the audience for the reading of a telegram sent by California State Assemblyman John Burton (D-San Francisco). The telegram conveyed Burton's "unhappiness with the manner in which the San Francisco Housing Authority treats its tenants." Citing the FEPC report, he accused the administration of being "totally lacking not only in the understanding of the purpose of public housing laws, but also inept in its day-to-day functions." Burton recommended that the commission "find a new Secretary who is not only well versed as to public housing but also has an understanding and feeling for the needs of people." He emphasized that the SFHA had to have a "full commitment to human dignity and equality." Although some SFHA staff defended Beard and the housing program, the evidence and opposition was too great. John Beard stepped down after twenty-two years at the SFHA helm.

Kane and the commissioners produced a manual . . . to reduce discrimination and better integrate San Francisco's neighborhoods.

In John Beard's place, San Francisco Mayor John Shelley appointed his aide and friend Eneas Kane to administer the seven-thousand-unit program. Born and educated in the city, Kane had attended law school at the University of San Francisco with Shelley, then taught English, public speaking, and social ethics at Saint Ignatius High School and the University of San Francisco. From 1936 to his SFHA appointment in October 1965, the tall, red-headed Kane was in public relations in the private and public sector. Kane brought a friendlier style to the position. SFHA Commissioner Stephen Walter conceded that Kane "might lack some technical knowledge," but that on the whole, he felt Kane was "well qualified in the field of housing" and thought "his well-known sympathies for matters of civil rights will be able to help us immeasurably." In contrast to the SFHA leaders of the 1950s, Kane and the commissioners were committed to public housing. Part of this commitment came from the historic failure of the private sector. SFHA Commissioner Hamilton Boswell, minister of Jones Methodist Church, noted that only public housing had ensured "real security" to low-income families. "Unless we have public housing," he said, "poor people do not stand a chance to remain in the Western Addition, Hunters Point, or anywhere else." Kane believed public housing was absolutely necessary because "the private housing sector has not to date been able to solve the housing problems of San Francisco and other urban areas."

Kane was committed to a "new approach to the authority's dual obligation to its tenants and the people of San Francisco." That approach, he said, would focus on "the twin goals of reorganization within and reaching out beyond." His internal reorganization cut administration costs, clarified SFHA staff duties, and improved staff morale. At the urging of tenants and civil rights organizations, Kane and the commissioners produced a manual for SFHA staff to reduce discrimination and better integrate San Francisco's neighborhoods. They also used the authority's contracts to break down racial barriers in union apprenticeship programs and hiring halls, though progress on this issue moved at a glacial pace. In his area of expertise, Kane used radio, newspaper, and television coverage to repair the authority's tarnished image. Although they worked under many constraints, SFHA officials were civic leaders committed to using the housing authority to meet the housing and social needs of the city's residents.

The Nixon Presidency and Tenant Activism

The [Richard M.] Nixon administration wreaked havoc on the [National Association of Housing and Redevelopment Officials]. As (NAHRO) president and secretary of one of the nation's largest authorities, Kane understood the scope of the public housing crisis. At the 1971 NAHRO conference, he criticized the administration's priorities and the half-truths about congressional spending ceilings. The "administration," he said, "has chosen to spend funds for trips to the moon, national defense and many other things rather than to spend the funds for public housing." In addition to not releasing funds to local authorities, the HUD formula for maintenance and administration continued to force authorities to burn up their reserves. After hearing a report on housing legislation, SFHA Commissioner Caroline Charles complained, "I have felt for quite some time that we are being driven out of business, and I think it is ultimately going to happen." The core problem, she said, was that HUD officials expected authorities to break even or be "profitable," even though public housing "was established to be a subsidized operation. There is something very different between those two ideas." As the discussion of the report continued, Commissioner Walter put it bluntly: "We all know that housing is being phased out by the Executive Branch of this Government." The impulse to dismantle social and civil rights programs came from a growing body of antistatist knowledge and a grassroots movement funded and organized by whites. These activities had a noticeable effect on policy makers at all government levels, who turned these ideas into public policies.

Tenants bore the brunt of these policies. Not every tenant believed that "rent was theft" or called for a "socialist city structure"; nor did every tenant see the struggle as part of the liberation movements around the globe. But tenants and their allies constructed a political culture at odds with some city and national leaders and national trends of many white voters who were losing faith in an activist liberal government. Low-income tenants lived with the twin effects of unemployment and housing speculation. When tenants such as Cecilia Keough felt they were "caught in the vicious vise of brutal and heartless 'S.F. style Redevelopment,'" they knew that it was not just the hassle of moving but the lack of housing and job options that made urban renewal so hard to accept. Tenants wrote letters, organized rent strikes and sit-ins, and used direct action to raise their consciousness much in the same way that job struggles raised worker consciousness. Struggles over redevelopment and public housing policy radicalized participants and constructed political identities around their tenancy and place. In private housing, the more radical tenant unions were revolting against property owners. . . .

Nonwhites and women especially worked on making public lic housing policies square with political traditions of equality and justice.

Activists and Political Gains

Public housing tenants had high expectations for their program. SFHA tenants wanted a say in everything from the color of doors in modernization projects to having representation on the SFHA commission. Although some theorists would interpret tenant organizing as interest-group politics, it is better understood in terms of ordinary people's wanting to control the public and private policies that affected their homes and communities. It fit into a citywide movement based on their experiences with private and public landlords and employers, both of whom had wielded a disproportionate amount of power over them. Nonwhites and women especially worked on making public housing policies square with political traditions of equality and justice. They used the SFHA to break down barriers in housing and jobs and organized around an expanded vision of rights, their status as tenants, and their housing struggles. These struggles contributed to and built on the other social movements of the period in and out of the city.

They continued to educate, advise, and organize.

For almost a decade, tenants and civic groups had asked for tenant appointments to the SFHA commission. Since the creation of the housing program, mayors had appointed friends, friends of a friend, or community leaders who had much different life experiences than public housing tenants. The program suffered as a result. Tenants called into question the legitimacy of the program and used their unions to put collective pressure on the SFHA leadership. In August 1973, the SFHA commission expanded to seven, adding two tenants who were elected by their peers but still appointed by the mayor. The first two tenant commissioners were Martin Helpman and Cleo Wallace. Commissioner Amancio Ergina welcomed Wallace and Helpman, remarking that "their interest in the community and city is well known. Their record of individual accomplishment is a source of pride to our community and our country." In theory, the new commissioners represented all the tenants, but in practice, Helpman had closer ties to seniors, Wallace to families. The appointments represented an important development for the SFHA as nontenant commissioners learned from tenant commissioners and tenants gained two advocates who understood and identified with the city's public-housing tenant community.

Tenant commissioners took their position seriously. Wallace and Helpman regularly toured SFHA housing and discussed both small and large problems with tenants. They continued to educate, advise, and organize. Tenants turned to Wallace and Helpman for assistance first. This was illustrated in 1973 when the Redevelopment Agency bulldozers were on the verge of destroying 196 permanent public housing units in

Hunters Point. The tenants, however, refused to leave because they did not believe HUD assurances that subsidized housing would be available. Others, including a few commissioners, worried that this was the first step toward demolishing other public housing in the district. At a contentious and emotional commission meeting, Wallace spoke against the bulldozers and read a prayer by a tenant: "Our father in Heaven, We Pray you save us from the Man's evil bulldozers. The houses you have given the oppressed and poor are being taken the World over by evil doers. H.U.D. Redevelopment says destruction must come for their own selfish gains. The politician has let us down for False Gods of money and power. Forgive the politicians, Lord. Redevelopment has confused the world with destruction in our land. Our destiny we do not know with bulldozers coming sooner than we think. Children are asking where are we going?" The other commissioners and Kane sided with the tenants, even though Mayor Alioto's office and the Redevelopment Agency were "vehemently in favor of demolition."

Divides Between the City and Public Housing Activists

The SFHA and its tenants were unable to stop the bulldozers, nor did they get funding for additional public housing. The SFHA leadership stood by the tenants because it, like the tenants, knew there were very few housing units in the city. The waiting list for public and subsidized housing remained long. In 1975, the authority operated forty-three permanent projects with a total of 7,132 units and managed roughly 1,200 Section 23 units. Family housing remained particularly tight in both public and subsidized housing. In a report to the commissioners, Kane noted that "not one single unit of new housing had been built in San Francisco by private enterprise in the last 15 to 20 years that our clients could afford." SFHA construction of family units, too, had slowed, and the quality of its larger units suffered from budget cuts, which in 1975 caused Kane to eliminate seventy jobs from an already bare-bones maintenance staff.

Redevelopment and reductions in maintenance staff ensured an active tenant population. Although rent strikes and threats of rent strikes were less common, tenants found that a collective voice drew the fastest response from the SFHA staff, and they relied on their associations to get small and large repairs done. In addition to bargaining with the authority, tenant unions continued to provide an important source of power for tenants. For example, the SFPHA worked with a coalition of one hundred city organizations and turned out tenants for a rally on the first of March, 1975, against an increase in food stamp costs. Whether at the project or city level, tenant unions protected social services and continued to put representatives on committees that decided jobs, contracts, and community issues. Tenants worked together to improve their housing, assist SFHA staff with HUD policies, and stage cultural events and political actions. As they did this, they constructed their housing, their community, and their identity.

Organizations to Contact

The editors have compiled the following list of organizations concerned with the issues debated in this book. The descriptions are derived from materials provided by the organizations. All have publications or information available for interested readers. The list was compiled on the date of publication of the present volume; the information provided here may change. Be aware that many organizations take several weeks or longer to respond to inquiries, so allow as much time as possible.

Cato Institute
1000 Massachusetts Ave., N.W., Washington, DC   20001
(202) 842-0200 • fax (202) 842 3490
e-mail: pr@cato.org
Web site: www.cato.org

The Cato Institute, a nonprofit, libertarian public-policy research center, was founded in 1977 by Edward H. Crane. The institute promotes limited government, free enterprise and individual choice. The Cato Institute sponsors seminars and conferences on public policy, and it publishes a variety of materials, many of which are available on its Web site. The Institute provides information on libertarian activism, including grassroots initiatives at the local and state level.

Common Cause
1133 19th Street, NW, 9th Floor, Washington, DC   20036
(202) 833-1200
e-mail: grassroots@commoncause.org
Web site: www.commoncause.org

Common Cause is a nonprofit, nonpartisan, advocacy group founded in 1970 with the goal of holding elected officials accountable to the American people. Common Cause promotes a variety of activist causes, such as campaign finance reform, voter registration drives, and openness in government. The organization has chapters in thirty-six states and more than 300,000 members. Its Web site has an archive of its online journal, *Common Cause Magazine,* as well as links to its publications, including research papers, press releases, and blogs.

The Conservative Caucus
450 Maple Ave East, Vienna, VA   22180
(703) 938-9626
Web site: www.conservativeusa.org

The Conservative Caucus (TCC) was founded in 1974 by Howard Phillips, the leader of the conservative Constitution Party (formerly the United States Taxpayers Party). The TCC emphasizes grassroots efforts at the local and state level as part of a larger strategy to promote conservative principles in American politics. The TCC often organizes letter-writing, e-mail, and telephone campaigns on national and state legislation. The organization's Web site describes itself as a conservative activist's "toolbox" and contains a variety of information and strategies to help grassroots initiatives.

Democratic National Committee
430 South Capitol St., S.E., Washington, DC   20003
(202) 863-8000
Web site: www.democrats.org

The Democratic National Committee (DNC) is the governing body of the Democratic Party in the United States, one of the two main political parties in the country. The partisan organization provides information on major national and state issues from the party's perspective. It also offers details on how to get involved in political campaigns and liberal activist causes. The DNC web site examines contemporary legislation and legal issues from a Democratic perspective. It also provides information about the party organization and structure.

Earth Foundation
5401 Mitchelldale, Suite B-4, Houston, TX   77092
(800) 566-6539 • fax (713) 686-6561

e-mail: monkey@earthfound.com
Web site: www.earthfound.com

Created in 1990, the Earth Foundation is a grassroots organization that emphasizes education and preservation. The Foundation provides educational tools for teachers and students. It endeavors to show students how they can make a difference on environmental matters. The Foundation's network now includes more than ten thousand schools across the country, and it sponsors campaigns to save specific areas in the United States or abroad from development through its Adopt-an-Acre program in which participating school systems purchase an average of ten acres to set aside for preservation.

Environmental Defense
1875 Connecticut Ave., NW, Suite 600
Washington, DC   20009
(800) 684-3322
e-mail: members@environmentaldefense.org
Web site: www.environmentaldefense.org

Environmental Defense (ED) is a nonpartisan, nonprofit organization that endeavors to promote environmental rights for all people, including clean air and water, healthy food and ecosystems. ED has more than 500,000 members (400,000 in the United States), and it seeks to influence policy at the national level through research and lobbying and at the state and local level through activism. The organization constantly seeks volunteers and professionals to bolster its efforts and it distributes action alerts via e-mail, and texts to coordinate its supporters.

Feminist Majority Foundation
1600 Wilson Boulevard, Suite 801, Arlington, VA   22209
(703) 522-2214 • fax (703) 522-2219
Web site: www.feminist.org

The Feminist Majority Foundation (FMF) was founded in 1987 to promote women's social, legal, and political equality. The organization combines research on policy issues and direct activism. Through its publications, the FMF seeks to educate men and women about inequality and solutions to discrimination. The FMF also attempts to educate the next generation of American women leaders. The organization undertakes a variety of direct action, including grassroots organizing projects in states and localities, and sponsors forums on gender issues and empowerment.

National Partnership for Women and Families
1875 Connecticut Ave, NW, Suite 650
Washington, DC   20009
(202) 986-2600 • fax (202) 986-2539
e-mail: info@nationalpartnership.org
Web site: www.nationalpartnership.org

Originally founded in 1971 as the Women's Legal Defense Fund, the organization expanded its focus to include family issues and in 1998 became the National Partnership for Women and Families. The Partnership concentrates on issues that affect women and families, such as healthcare, child support, gender discrimination, and both political and economic equality. The organization relies on activists and volunteers in local, state, and national campaigns that seek to influence legislation.

People for the Ethical Treatment of Animals (PETA)
501 Front Street, Norfolk, VA   23510
(757) 622-7382
Web site: www.peta.org

Founded in 1980, People for the Ethical Treatment of Animals (PETA) has developed a reputation for aggressively using direct activism to promote animal rights. PETA is a global nonprofit organization. With more than 1.6 million members, it is the largest animal rights group in the world. PETA undertakes investigative work and presents its findings to the public through education programs and media campaigns. The organization sponsors demonstrations and protests, consumer boycotts, letter and e-mail campaigns, and governmental action.

Project Vote Smart
One Common Ground, Philipsburg, MT 59858
(888) 868 3762
e-mail: comments@vote-smart.org
Web site: www.vote-smart.org

Project Vote Smart is a nonprofit, nonpartisan organization that seeks to increase voter participation in the United States through education. The Project utilizes volunteers to conduct a National Political Awareness Test (NPAT) prior to each election and publishes its findings. NPAT provides a means to learn candidates' positions on various national issues and serves as a voting guide and informational tool for the press. The Project also maintains biographical information on candidates and comparisons between of officials' voting records and their public stance on issues.

Reform Party
P.O. Box 3236, Abilene, TX 79604
(325) 672-2575
e-mail: info@reformparty.org
Web site: www.reformparty.org

The Reform Party was founded in 1995 by Ross Perot, who ran for the presidency in 1992, and again in 1996. The populist organization stresses responsible government, term limits, and a balanced federal budget. It was organized by grassroots activists unhappy with the nation's dominant two-party system. The party's Web site has its platform and links to state organizations, overviews of candidates, and other political organizations. It also provides information on how citizens can become involved in local politics.

Republican National Committee
310 1st St., S.E., Washington, DC 20003
(202) 863-8500
Web site: www.gop.com

The Republican National Committee (RNC) is the governing body of the Republican Party (also known as the Grand Old Party or GOP). As one of the two main partisan political par-

117

ties in the United States, the RNC provides a forum for individuals to become involved in conservative activism. The RNC coordinates the national campaigns of the party and offers support to state and local chapters. The party's Web site provides information on national and state issues. The site also details the GOP's history, structure, and organization.

Bibliography

Books

Deborah Barndt   *Wild Fire: Art as Activism*. Toronto: Sumach Press, 2006.

Bruce Bimber and   *Campaigning Online: The Internet in*
Richard Davis   *U.S. Elections*. New York: Oxford University Press, 2003.

Yvonne Bynoe   *Stand and Deliver: Political Activism, leadership and Hip Hop Culture*. Brooklyn: Soft Skull Press, 2004.

Andrea Louise   *How Policies Make Citizens: Senior*
Campbell   *Political Activism and the American Welfare State*. Princeton: Princeton University Press, 2003.

Andrew Chadwick   *Internet Politics: States, Citizens, and New Communication Technologies*. New York: Oxford University Press, 2006.

Melissa Checker   *Local Actions: Cultural Activism,*
and Maggie   *Power, and Public Life in America*.
Fishman, eds.   New York: Columbia University Press, 2004.

Eldridge Cleaver.   *Target Zero: A Life in Writing*. New
Ed. by Kathleen   York: Palgrave Macmillan, 2006.
Cleaver

Steve Davis	*Click on Democracy: The Internet's Power to Change Political Apathy into Civic Action.* Boulder, CO: Westview, 2002.
Dana R. Fisher	*Activism, Inc.: How the Outsourcing of Grassroots Campaigns Is Strangling Progressive Politics in America.* Stanford: Stanford University Press, 2006.
Dianne D. Glave and Mark Stoll, eds.	*To Love the Wind and the Rain: African Americans and Environmental History.* Pittsburgh: University of Pittsburgh Press, 2006.
Mary E. Hawksworth	*Globalization and Feminist Activism.* Lanham, MD: Rowman & Littlefield, 2006.
Harry Henderson	*Campaign and Election Reform.* New York: Facts on File, 2004.
David Hostetter	*Movement Matters: American Antiapartheid Activism and the Rise of Multicultural Politics.* New York: Routledge, 2006.
Philip N. Howard	*New Media Campaigns and the Managed Citizen.* New York: Cambridge University Press, 2006.
Gayle Kimball, ed.	*Women's Culture in a New Era: A Feminist Revolution?* Lanham, MD: Scarecrow Press, 2005.
Jama Lazerow and Yohuru Williams, eds.	*In Search of the Black Panther Party: New Perspectives on a Revolutionary Movement.* Durham: Duke University Press, 2006.

Martha   *Latinos in a Changing Society.* West-
Montero-Sieburth   port, CT: Praeger, 2007.
and Edwin
Melendez

Lyle Munro   *Compassionate Beasts: The Quest for Animal Rights.* Westport, CT: Praeger, 2001.

Ralph Nader   *Crashing the Party: Taking on the Corporate Government in an Age of Surrender.* New York: St. Martin's 2002.

Pippa Norris   *Democratic Phoenix: Reinventing Political Activism.* New York: Cambridge University Press, 2002.

Karen L. Riley, ed. *Social Reconstruction: People, Politics, Perspectives.* Greenwich, CT: Information Age Pub., 2006.

Jessica Singer   *Stirring Up Justice: Writing and Reading to Change the World.* Portsmouth, NH: Heinemann, 2006.

Craig Smith   *Sing My Whole Life Long: Jenny Vincent's Life in Folk Music and Activism.* Albuquerque: University of New Mexico Press, 2007.

Joe Trippi   *The Revolution Will Not be Televised: Democracy, the Internet, and the Overthrow of Everything.* New York: ReganBooks, 2004.

Robert Weissberg   The *Limits of Civic Activism: Cautionary Tales on the Use of Politics.* New Brunswick, NJ: Transaction Publishers, 2005.

Periodicals

Andrew Achenbaum
"A History of Civic Engagement of Older People," *Generations*, Winter 2006.

Scott Bradner
"'Net as a Political Tool, Almost a Joke," *Network World*, April 10, 2006.

Philip Brit
"The 'Net Effect' on Political Campaign Strategy," *Information Today*, June 2007.

Elizabeth Cherry
"Veganism as a Cultural Movement," *Social Movement Studies*. September 2006.

Jen Christiansen
"Jeff vs. the Bloggers," *Advocate* May 10, 2005.

The Economist
"Owner Drivers: Activist Investors," June 2, 2005.

Laura Flanders
"Bottom-Up Power: Grassroots Dems Take Back Politics from the Politicians," *The Nation*, April 23, 2007.

Futurist
"Making Activism Work," May–June 2002.

Lawrence Goldenhersh
"Red State, Blue State, Internet State," *Environmental Protection*, January–February 2007.

Gwen Gregory
"The Political System Goes Online: The Internet Is Quickly Becoming an Important Factor in U.S. Politics," *Information Today*, October 1, 2002.

Elen Griffiths   "Why I Became a Teenage Eco-
                    Warrior," *Times Educational Supple-
                    ment*, September 16, 2005.

David Korten   "Build the Alliances," *Yes*, Spring
                    2005.

Anna Kuchment   "It's Hip to Be Green: Activism,"
                    Newsweek, April 16, 2007.

Newsweek   "The Greening of America," August
International   14, 2006.

Thomas Parris   "Sustainable Development in the Bl-
                    ogosphere," *Environment*, May 2005.

Joseph E. Peniel   "Black Power's Powerful Legacy,"
                    Chronicle of Higher Education, July
                    21, 2006.

Christopher   "The New SDS," *Nation*, April 16,
Phelps   2007.

Tom Price   "The New Environmentalism: Era of
                    Activism," *CQ Researcher*, December
                    1, 2006.

Matthew   "Protestor=Criminal?" *The Progres-*
Rothschild   *sive*, February 2004.

Jonathan Schell   "Thinking Movement, Working
                    Demonstration," *Nation*, June 23,
                    2003.

Searcher   "All Politics Is Local? The Rise of
                    National Political Communities," Oc-
                    tober 2006.

Paul Starr   "Political Networking," *Technology Review*, April 2005.

Robert Weissberg   "Abandoning Politics," *Society*, May–June 2004.

Belinda Wheaton   "Identity, Politics, and the Beach: Environmental Activism in Surfers Against Sewage," *Leisure Studies*, July 2007.

Index

A

Action alerts, 46
Activism
    animal rights, 86–93
    contemporary, 70–71
    dramatic affect of student, 62–71
    education and, 66–67
    government should not support, 22–32
    government should support, 12–21
    Internet, 7–11, 45–61
    outsourced, 38–44
    social learning and, 67
    tenant, 103–112
    terrorism and, 86–93
    waning of student, 72–74
    See also Environmental activism; Grassroots activism
Activists, extreme measures used by, 85–93
AmeriCorps, 15–18, 20
Anderson, Marc, 39
Animal Enterprise Protection Act, 92
Animal rights activists, use of violence by, 86–93
Apollo Alliance, 76–77
Armies of compassion, 15, 17, 31
Aviv, Diana, 31

B

Bachrach, Taylor, 48–49, 50
Baranski, John, 103
Beard, John, 105, 106
Beinecke, Frances, 84

Bennett Environmental Inc., 46–47
Berger, Peter, 14–15
Bibi, Mark, 86
Blackwelder, Brent, 77, 78
Blogforamerica.com, 8, 55
Blogs, political, 8, 55
Bowling Alone (Putnam), 14
Bridgeland, John M., 12
Burleigh, Alma, 105
Burton, John, 106
Bush administration
    environmental movement and, 77–80, 84
    promotion of civic engagement by, 12–13, 15–21
    support of faith-based organizations by, 22–27

C

California State University system, 63–64
Campaign contributions, raising, on Web, 9–10, 54, 56
Campaign workers
    functions of, 35–36
    importance of, 34–35
    professional, 57–60
Canvassers, for outsourced activism, 40–42, 44
Canvassing activities, 35, 39
Carney, Eliza Newlin, 22
Carter, Jimmy, 51
Catholic Charities USA, 25, 29
Charitable choice model, 25–26

Charity, Aid, Recovery, and Empowerment (CARE) Act, 26–27, 31

Charles, Caroline, 108

Christian Coalition, 42

Citizen participation, 96–99

Citizen Service Act, 18–19

Citizens Corp, 13

Citizenship, 96–97

Civic agenda, of Bush administration, 12–21

Civic disengagement, increased, 14

Civil Rights Act, 98

Civil rights movement, 81–82

Clean Water Action, 39

Climate change, 80–81

Clinton, Bill, 25, 79

College students, activism among. *See* Student activism

Colorado, 83

Communicopia.net, 48–49

"Communities of Character" initiative, 15

Community, decline of, 14

Conservative agenda, grassroots activism for, 42–43

Contemporary activism, 70–71

Cornfield, Michael, 51

Cornuelle, Richard, 14

D

D'Amelio, Laura, 45

Dean, Howard, 7–11, 51–56

Dean Scream, 10

Dean Wireless, 9

DeanforAmerica.com, 7–8, 52–54

Deaniacs, 7

DeanLink, 54–56

DeanRocks.com, 8

Democracy, political activism and, 14

Democratic National Committee, 35, 41

Democratic Party, outsourcing trend in, 41–43

Digital divide, 49–50

Dillenback, Sally, 90–91

Dilulio, John, Jr., 23–24

Direct action, 87

Disposable people, 63

E

Economic disparities, 62–63

Education

activism and, 66–67

social learning and, 67

Election campaigns. *See* Political campaigns

Election Day, 34–37

Election officials, 36–37

Email spam, 49

Environmental activism

of 1960s and 1970s, 81–83

at community level, 94–102

decline in, 78–80

diversification of, 76–77

has been crucial for movement, 75–84

politics and, 77–80

at state and local level, 80–84

use of Internet in, 45–50

See also specific organizations

Environmental justice groups, 80, 95–102

Environmental Protection Agency (EPA), 98–101

Environmental racism, 98–102

Extremism, by animal rights activists, 86–93

F

Faith-based organizations
  accountability issues with,
    30–31
  Bush administration's support
    for, 22–27
  defining, 28
  intermediaries and, 29–31
  lack of new funding for,
    31–32
  problems with, 24, 27
  traditional funding for, 25
Federal grants, to states, 29
Fisher, Dana R., 38
Florida, 84
Foreign oil, reduced dependency
  on, 76–77
France, student demonstrations in,
  73–74
Freedom Corps. *See* USA Freedom
  Corps
Friends of the Earth, 77
Frigault, Allain, 47
Fuller, Millard, 17
Fund for Public Interest Research,
  40–41
Fundraising, Web-based, 9–10, 54,
  56

G

General Electric, 80
Global warming, 80–81
Goldsmith, Stephen, 12
Gore, Al, 80
Government
  should not support activism,
    22–32
  should support activism,
    12–21

Government funding, lack of additional, for social service programs, 31–32
Grassroots activism
  decline of, to outsourced ac-
    tivism, 38–40
  Internet and, 7–11, 45–61
  is key to successful political
    campaigns, 33–37
  is most effective, 94–102
  nonpartisan, 36
  organizing strategies for,
    68–69
  by Republican Party, 42–43
  roots of, 39
  should work with local offi-
    cials, 103–112
Great Society programs, 104
Greenpeace, 43–44, 45–46
Guinane, Kay, 30

H

Habitat for Humanity, 17–18
Harlos, Marion, 89–90
Harris, Katherine, 84
Health and Human Services
  (HHS) Department, 29–30
Heaven, Sally Green, 40
Helpman, Martin, 110
Hertsgaard, Mark, 75
HHS Compassion Capital Fund,
  30, 31
Hicks, Karen, 41–42
Housing and Urban Development
  Department (HUD), 28, 104
Hunter, Bridget, 33
Huntingdon Life Sciences (HSL),
  86–87, 88–93
Hurricane Katrina, 80

I

Illegal acts, by activists, 85–93
Independent Sector, 31
Inhofe, James, 87
Internet
    fundraising, 9–10, 54, 56
    has revolutionized politics,
        45–50
    political campaigns and, 7–11,
        51–61
Intimidation, by animal rights
    activists, 89–91
Issue-based canvassing, 39

J

Johnson, Lyndon B., 104
Jones, Elise, 83
Jones, Van, 81–82

K

Kane, Eneas, 106–108
Kerry, John F., 7, 10
King, Martin Luther, Jr., 70
Kinney, Catherine, 86
Kriess-Tomkins, Jonathan, 54–55
Kurtz, Hilda, 94

L

League of Women Voters, 36
Lenkowsky, Leslie, 12
Lewis, John, 87–88
Life Sciences Research (LSR),
    86–87
Literature drops, 35
Local officials, grassroots activism
    and, 103–112
Louisiana Department of Environ-
    mental Quality (LDEQ), 102
Lugo, Luis, 27

Lukashenko, Aleksandr, 74

M

Mailers, 35
Marsh, 89–91
Marx, Gary, 43
Mass demonstrations
    in France, 73–74
    utility of, 74
McIntosh, Brent, 92
MeetUp.com, 8–9, 54
Message development, 57–58
Michigan, 83–84
Miller, John J., 85
Modern world, problems in,
    62–63
Mogus, Jason, 48, 49
Moskowitz, Laurie, 43
MoveOn.org, 56

N

Narrowcasting, 49
National Association of Housing
    and Redevelopment Officials
    (NAHRO), 108
National service programs
    Bush's support of, 13
    role of government in sup-
        porting, 17–21
    See also specific programs
National Wildlife Federation,
    75–76
Nelson, Mary, 31–32
Neuhaus, Richard John, 14–15
New York Stock Exchange (NYSE),
    85–87
Newkirk, Ingrid, 86
Nixon, Richard M., 108
Nonpartisan volunteers, 36
Nordhaus, Ted, 78

O

Omatsu, 62
OMB Watch, 30
Operation Blessing International, 29–30
Orrell, Brent, 29
Outsourced activism, problems with, 38–44

P

Paddock, Mary Louise, 105–106
Parish, Billy, 80–81
Parker, Buck, 82
Passacantando, John, 40, 43–44
Peace Corps, 16, 20
Pennington, Doug, 72
People
    disposable, 63
    educating, about social problems, 66–67
    empowerment of, 14–15
    social learning by, 67
Perna, Elaine, 91
Phone-banking, 35
Policy campaign market, 59
Political activism. See Activism
Political campaigns
    grassroots organizations are key to, 33–37
    of Howard Dean, 7–11, 51–56
    Internet and, 7–11, 51–61
    outsourced activism and, 38–44
    professional, 57–60
    role of volunteers in, 34–37
Political organizing, 68–69
Political outsourcing, 38–44
Politics
    environmental movement and, 77–80

Internet activism has revolutionized, 45–50
    student activism has dramatically affected, 62–71
Pollack, Lana, 83–84
Pope, Carl, 82
Praxis, 64–65
Presidential campaign (2004)
    in Colorado, 83
    environmental movement and, 77–80
    grassroots activism during, 7–11, 42–43
    of Howard Dean, 7–11, 51–56
Privacy issues, with Internet, 49
Professional campaign workers, 57–60
Profit motive, 70
Progressive organizations
    need for local support by, 81–82
    outsourced activism by, 39–44
Property damage, by animal rights activists, 88
Putnam, Robert, 14

R

Racial diversity, in environmental movement, 76–77
Racism, environmental, 98–102
Reagan, Ronald, 79
Reclaiming the American Dream (Cornuelle), 14
Religious organizations. See Faith-based organizations
Republican National Committee, 35
Republican Party, grassroots activism by, 42–43
Republicans for Environmental Protection, 77
Richardson, Bill, 77

Ringo, Jerome, 75–77
Robertson, Pat, 29

S

San Francisco Housing Authority
(SFHA), 104–112
San Francisco, public housing ac-
tivism in, 103–112
Search for Common Ground USA,
28
Sellers, John, 78–79
Senior Corps, 16, 17, 20
September 1, 2001, increase in
civic engagement after, 13, 15–16
"72-Hour Plan," 42–43
Shellenberger, Michael, 78
Shelter in Place policy, 101
Shintech, Inc., 94–102
Sierra Club, 48
Social change
strategies for, 68–69
student activism's role in,
63–71
Social learning, 67
Social problems, mediating struc-
tures for dealing with, 14–15
Solmonese, Joe, 40
Spam, 49–50
St. James Citizens group, 95–102
St. James Parish, Louisiana, com-
munity activism in, 94–102
States
environmental movement and,
80–84
federal grants to, 29
Stop Huntingdon Animal Cruelty
(SHAC), 88–93
Strategic alliances, 64–65
Student activism
on environmental issues,
80–81

in France, 73–74
has had dramatic effect, 62–71
has waned, 72–74
Students in Free Enterprise
(SIFE), 18

T

Tanner, Michael, 28–29
Taylor, Betsy, 81
Tenant activism, 103–112
Tenpas, Kathryn Dunn, 24
Terrorism, 86–93
Text messaging, 9
Tocqueville, Alexis de, 14
Towey, Jim, 22–23, 30
Trippi, Joe, 8
Trull, Frankie, 88–89
Turgano, Rex, 47–48

U

University of Cincinnati Bearcat
Transportation System, 72–73
USA Freedom Corps, 13, 19–20

V

Value transformation, 70–71
Violence, use of by activists, 85–93
Vlasak, Jerry, 92
Volunteer organizations
faith-based, 22–32
government should not support, 22–32
promotion of, by government,
12–21
See also Grassroots activism;
specific organizations
Volunteers in Service to America
(VISTA), 18
Volunteers, role of in political
campaigns, 34–37

W

Wachs, Josh, 41
Wallace, Cleo, 110–111
Wal-Mart, 80
Web sites
    political campaign, 7–11,
    52–54
    See also Internet
Wendlandt, Wendy, 78
Workforce Investment Act, 29
Working Group on Human Needs
    and Faith-Based and Community
    Initiatives, 28

World problems, 62–63

Y

Yancey, Gaynord, 24
Young activists, importance of, 67
Young voters, appeal of Dean for,
    7–8

Z

Zwick, David, 39